CROCHET AMIGURUMI

YOU WILL BE ABLE TO CROCHET AMIGURUMI BY THE END OF THIS BOOK

FAY LYTH

ilex

CONTENTS

Introduction	6
What is Amigurumi?	8

YARNS, HOOKS & OTHER EQUIPMENT — 10

Crochet Hooks — 12
- Hook styles — 12
- Hook materials — 12
- Hook sizes — 13
- Which hook size to use — 13

Yarn — 15
- Yarn fibre — 15
- Yarn weight — 16
- Reading the yarn band or ball wrapper — 16
- Which yarn to use — 17

Additional Materials — 19
- Other tools and equipment — 19

READING A CROCHET PATTERN — 20
- Getting started — 22
- US vs UK terminology — 22
- Rows and rounds — 23
- Abbreviations and other terminology — 23
- Parentheses, brackets and asterisks — 24
- Sample pattern — 25
- Gauge/tension — 26
- Wrong side vs right side of amigurumi — 27

STITCHES, TECHNIQUES & FINISHING — 28

Crochet Basics — 30
- Holding your hook — 31
- Creating a slip knot — 32
- Holding your yarn — 34

Crochet Stitches and Other Techniques — 36
- Working the chain stitch (ch) — 36
- Counting chain stitches — 37
- Where to insert your hook — 37
- Working single crochet (sc) into a foundation chain — 38
- Working single crochet (sc) in rows — 40
- Yarn over vs yarn under — 41
- Turning chain (tch) — 42
- Crocheting around a foundation chain — 43
- Half double crochet (hdc) — 44
- Double crochet (dc) — 46
- Treble crochet (tr) — 48
- Slip stitch (sl st) — 52
- Working crochet in rounds — 53
- Counting stitches and rounds — 54
- Magic ring (mr) — 55
- Working an increase (inc) — 59
- Decrease (dec or sc2tog) — 60
- Invisible decrease (invdec) — 61
- Alternating increases and decreases — 62
- Changing colours — 63
- Working into the front loop only or back loop only — 64
- Joining yarn in unworked front loops — 65
- Crocheting an amigurumi piece closed — 66
- Crocheting amigurumi pieces together — 68

Finishing Techniques — 72
- Stuffing — 72
- Fastening off — 73
- Sewing techniques — 76
- Weaving in yarn ends — 81
- Adding facial details — 84

PATTERNS 90

Potato
92

Sour Lemon
96

Pencil
100

Planet
104

Mallard Duck
108

Mouse
112

Takeaway Coffee Cup
116

Hanging Cherries
120

Acorn
124

Ice Cream Cone
128

Bee
132

Octopus
138

Cat
142

Flower Pot
148

Bear
152

Index	158
Resources	160

INTRODUCTION

Welcome to the wonderful world of amigurumi!

Whether you've just picked up a crochet hook for the first time or you're looking for a fun new project, this book is the perfect place to start. At first glance, amigurumi may seem intimidating, but with just a hook, some yarn and a few simple stitches, you'll be whipping up your own adorable creations in no time.

I've dabbled in many crafts over the years – sewing, cross stitch, embroidery, jewellery making – but crochet is the one that has stuck with me the longest. There's something so satisfying about turning a length of yarn into something cute!

I began my crochet journey back in 2012. However, I had unsuccessfully tried teaching myself to crochet a few years prior, so don't get discouraged if it doesn't click straight away.

If you've never picked up a hook before, here's one piece of advice that I wish someone had told me: **there is no right or wrong way to crochet**. You don't have to hold your hook or yarn the same way as everyone else. As you're working through this book, I encourage you to try different things and find what works best for you, even if that means developing your own technique.

As with learning any new skill, **the key to success is practice and patience**. Have fun customizing your creations, embrace their quirks (it all adds to the handmade charm) and enjoy the creative journey.

I want this book to be a resource that you can continue to refer back to at any stage in your amigurumi journey, no matter your skill level. We'll cover the basic skills and techniques before diving into an array of cute patterns to help you practice and build upon those skills.

Happy Crocheting,
Fay x

WHAT IS AMIGURUMI?

Amigurumi is the Japanese art of crocheting or knitting stuffed dolls, animals or other characters. The word 'amigurumi' is derived from a combination of the Japanese words 'ami', meaning crocheted or knitted, and 'nuigurumi', meaning stuffed doll.

Amigurumi are typically worked in circular rounds, as opposed to in flat rows, to create three-dimensional shapes that are then sewn together and stuffed. Traditionally, amigurumi are small, cute characters that come to life with playful details – whether it's an adorable cat or a cheerful coffee cup. They're perfect for gifting since there's a character to suit just about anyone, and because they work up quickly and only require small amounts of yarn, they make great stash-busting projects.

YARNS, HOOKS & OTHER EQUIPMENT

If you are new to crochet, you'll only need a few tools and some yarn to get started. In this section, you'll learn all about the basic kit required for making amigurumi.

CROCHET HOOKS

Crochet hooks come in a variety of styles, sizes and materials. While I recommend you start off with a basic metal crochet hook, feel free to try out a few different styles and materials to find out which one you like best. Your choice of crochet hook will ultimately come down to personal preference – what you find most comfortable to hold and easy to use.

Inline   Tapered

HOOK STYLES

There are two different styles of crochet hook: inline and tapered. Inline hooks and tapered hooks differ primarily in their shape and design of the head and throat.

- Inline hooks have a pointy head that doesn't extend beyond the shaft with a flatter throat that's the same width as the shaft.
- Tapered hooks have a rounded head that extends beyond the shaft and the throat gradually narrows towards the tip.

HOOK MATERIALS

Crochet hooks come in a variety of different materials, such as aluminium, stainless steel, bamboo, wood, plastic and resin.

- Aluminium crochet hooks are the most common – they're smooth, lightweight and allow the yarn to glide smoothly, making them great for speed.
- Wooden hooks are more porous and tend to grip the yarn more, which can give you more control over the yarn if you find it's slipping too easily.
- Bamboo hooks behave similarly to wooden hooks. However, they get smoother, and therefore faster, with time.
- Plastic hooks are more common when it comes to larger hook sizes. I don't recommend them in smaller sizes, as with the tight stitches required for amigurumi, they can often bend and break when too much pressure is applied.

When you're first starting out, an inexpensive metal hook will suffice, but as your crochet journey progresses, you may want to invest in ergonomic crochet hooks. Whereas a standard hook most often has a straight handle with an indentation for the thumb rest, an ergonomically shaped hook is designed with a larger handle that allows for a more comfortable grip. Some people find an ergonomic hook can help alleviate the hand pain that is sometimes associated with long crochet sessions. Investing in ergonomic tools may also improve the speed and quality of your crochet.

HOOK SIZES

Hook size is determined by the weight of yarn that you're using and the project you're making. Crochet hooks are labelled with a metric size in millimetres, which is the diameter of the shaft where the stitches are formed. As well as a metric size, crochet hooks also have an equivalent size in imperial given as both a letter and/or a number.

WHICH HOOK SIZE TO USE

As a beginner, it's always best to stick with whatever hook size is recommended in the pattern you're following, especially when it comes to making amigurumi. Amigurumi requires a tight, dense fabric to prevent any stuffing showing through, so the hook size required will likely be smaller than what is recommended on the yarn band. A smaller hook equals smaller stitches.

HOOK SIZES

Metric	US sizes	UK sizes
2.00mm	–	14
2.25mm	B-1	13
2.50mm	–	12
2.75mm	C-2	11
3.25mm	D-3	10
3.50mm	E-4	9
3.75mm	F-5	8
4.00mm	G-6	7
5.00mm	H-8	6
5.50mm	I-9	5
6.00mm	J-10	4
6.50mm	K-10.5	3
8.00mm	L-11	0
9.00mm	M-13	00
10.00mm	N-15	000
12.00mm	P-16	–

YARN

Choosing yarn is one of the most fun parts of any crochet project. However, with so much choice available, it can be quite overwhelming. There are two important criteria to consider when choosing yarn for amigurumi: fibre and weight.

> **TIP**
> When it comes to yarn colours, pick your favourite shades or just stick to those recommended for each project.

YARN FIBRE

There is a huge selection of different yarn fibres to choose from, ranging from natural cotton and hand-dyed wool to acrylic and other synthetics. Most amigurumi are made using either acrylic or cotton yarn, both of which are widely available and come in a vast range of colours.

I've listed some of the pros and cons of acrylic and cotton yarn, but as you practice and try different yarns for yourself, you'll likely develop a preference for one or the other.

All the projects in this book are made with Paintbox Yarns Cotton Aran; a medium-weight worsted (#4) or aran cotton yarn. If you decide to use a different brand of yarn, choose a medium-weight yarn that's not too fuzzy or fluffy as it will be easier for you to clearly see and count your stitches.

PROS	CONS
ACRYLIC	
• Durable	• Synthetic material
• Widely available	• Can feel rough or scratchy
• Reasonably priced	• Reduced stitch definition
• Comes in a large range of colours	• Tends to pill over time
• Easy to clean	
COTTON	
• Natural material	• Available in limited yarn weights
• Durable	• Can't be washed at high temperatures due to risk of shrinkage
• Widely available	
• Comes in a large range of colours	• Absorbent so amigurumi may take longer to dry when washed
• Easy to clean	
• Clear stitch definition	
• Minimal stretch so holds its shape well	• Not as reasonably priced as acrylic yarn

YARN WEIGHT CATEGORIES

Craft Yarn Council Standard	US	UK	AUSTRALIA
#0 Lace	Lace	1 ply	2 ply
#1 Super Fine	Fingering, Sock	2 ply, 3 ply	3 ply
#2 Fine	Sport, Baby	4 ply	5 ply
#3 Light	Light Worsted	DK (Double Knit)	8 ply
#4 Medium	Worsted	Aran	10 ply
#5 Bulky	Bulky	Chunky	12 ply
#6 Super Bulky	Super Bulky	Super Chunky	14 ply
#7 Jumbo	Jumbo, Roving	Ultra	16+ ply

YARN WEIGHT

The term yarn weight refers to the thickness of the strand of yarn, not the weight of the overall ball or skein. Yarn weight is important as it determines the size, texture and overall look of your finished project. If you use a yarn that's too thick or too fine for your pattern, you may end up with a crocheted fabric that's way bigger, smaller, floppier or tighter and harder to work with than you expected.

There is a name given to each weight of yarn, which can vary from country to country. In the US, yarn weight is sometimes represented by a number as well as a name, ranging from #0 to #7, where the finest yarns are #0 and the bulkiest yarns are #7. Within the same yarn weight category, there is always some variation across different brands, so keep this in mind if you're planning to mix a variety of yarns of the same weight within a single project.

READING THE BALL BAND OR YARN WRAPPER

The ball band or yarn wrapper is the label that comes around a ball or skein of yarn. It is where you'll find all the information about the yarn. If purchasing online, the information printed on the yarn band should also be included in the product listing.

TYPICAL YARN BAND

BRAND NAME AND YARN NAME: The name of the yarn manufacturer and the name of that specific yarn.

FIBRE: What material the yarn is made from. If it's a blend, it will list the relative content, for example: 50% cotton, 50% acrylic.

YARN WEIGHT: For example: lace, worsted/aran, bulky/chunky.

COLOUR: The name/number for that particular shade of yarn.

DYE LOT: The number assigned to that specific batch of yarn. Different dye lots can vary slightly in colour.

BALL WEIGHT: The amount of yarn in each ball or skein, given in ounces or grams.

YARDAGE: The length of yarn in each ball, given in yards or metres.

RECOMMENDED HOOK/NEEDLE SIZE: The recommended hook/needle size to achieve a specified number of stitches and/or rows with the yarn.

GAUGE/TENSION: This is a guide to the number of stitches and rows within a 4-inch (10-cm) square, usually measured over knitted stockinette/stocking stitch when using the recommended needle size.

CARE INSTRUCTIONS: The care symbols indicate how to launder your finished project, including washing, drying and ironing instructions or whether it needs to be dry cleaned.

WHICH YARN TO USE

When first starting out, I recommend sticking to the materials that are given at the start of the pattern. However, you may not have access to that particular brand of yarn or you might want to avoid buying new yarn and use up something you already have in your yarn stash. If so, here are the most important things to consider when substituting yarn for amigurumi:

Yarn weight

Most amigurumi patterns can be made using different yarns or even yarn weights, however, your end result will likely look different from the amigurumi shown in the photograph. For example: if you use a super bulky/chunky yarn with a larger size hook instead of a worsted/aran yarn with the recommended size hook, your finished project will be a lot bigger.

Hook size

Substituting yarns also affects the recommended hook size as finer yarns require a smaller hook and vice versa. When choosing the right hook for amigurumi, a good rule of thumb is to go down a full hook size than what is recommended on the ball band or yarn wrapper.

Yarn 17

ADDITIONAL MATERIALS

Some patterns will require small amounts of additional materials such as felt fabric, chenille stems/pipe cleaners, plastic or poly pellets, cardboard, fabric glue or other embellishments. Always check the pattern for the full list of materials needed.

OTHER TOOLS AND EQUIPMENT

Once you have your hook and yarn, there are a few other essential supplies that you'll need and a few others that are nice to have:

SCISSORS: Small sharp scissors are a must in any tool kit.

TAPE MEASURE: It's useful to keep a measuring tool on hand especially when making a project where gauge/tension is important.

PINS: Dressmaking pins are helpful for holding crocheted pieces together while sewing up, and for marking the placement of details.

EMBROIDERY FLOSS/THREAD: Available in an almost endless number of colours, embroidery floss is useful for adding features to your characters. The individual strands can be separated to allow for finer details.

EMBROIDERY NEEDLE: An embroidery needle with a sharp tip is useful for adding finer details. Look for one with a large eye to make it easier to thread.

YARN OR TAPESTRY NEEDLE: A yarn or tapestry needle is longer and thicker than a regular sewing needle. It usually has a blunt tip and a large eye for threading yarn. It is used to weave in yarn ends, stitch pieces together or add sewn embellishments. Choose metal needles over plastic as they're more durable and glide through the stitches easier.

STUFFING: Polyester fibre filling is the most popular choice for toy stuffing. Whatever toy stuffing you choose, make sure that it conforms to current fire safety standards.

SAFETY EYES: Safety eyes help bring your creations to life. They are available in a wide range of sizes and colours. They are made up of two pieces: the eye that sits on the outside of the piece and the washer that snaps onto the back to lock the eye safely in place. When using safety eyes, consider who the finished project is for, as safety eyes aren't suitable for children under the age of 3.

STITCH MARKERS: Usually small plastic or metal clasps that can be locked in place, stitch markers are used to mark the beginning of a new round. Alternatively, you can use hair/bobby pins, paper clips or even a piece of scrap yarn instead.

READING A CROCHET PATTERN

Being able to read a crochet pattern is a highly important skill and a key part of learning to crochet. While it can seem overwhelming at first, much like learning a new language, it's definitely worth putting in the time and effort as it will give you access to a whole new world of crochet.

GETTING STARTED

Before starting to crochet, always read through the pattern first, especially the key information given at the beginning. This usually includes the materials needed, finished size of the project, recommended gauge/tension, stitch abbreviations and any special stitches/terms, plus any extra notes about the pattern.

While there are certain common conventions when it comes to written crochet patterns, it's important to note that every designer has their own pattern writing style. As you gain experience, you'll start to recognize some similarities between patterns, but to help I have included a short guide to crochet terminology. Once you begin to recognize the most frequently used abbreviations, everything will start to make sense.

US VS UK TERMINOLOGY

The US and UK have different names for some of the same crochet stitches, as well as some overlap, which can be confusing. Because of this, even before you pick up your hook, it's crucial to check through the pattern first to determine whether US or UK terminology is being used.

NOTE

The patterns in this book are written using US terminology.

US TERMS	UK TERMS
chain (ch)	chain (ch)
slip stitch (sl st)	slip stitch (ss)
single crochet (sc)	double crochet (dc)
half double crochet (hdc)	half treble crochet (htr)
double crochet (dc)	treble crochet (tr)
treble/triple crochet (tr)	double treble crochet (dtr)

Reading a crochet pattern

ROWS AND ROUNDS

At the very start of a pattern, or at the beginning of a section, the instructions will state whether the piece is worked in rows or in rounds. The difference between rows and rounds is the direction that you crochet in. Whereas rows are worked flat by turning over the piece at the end of each row and crocheting back and forth in a line, rounds are worked in a continuous circular direction and the piece is never turned over. Both flat and cylindrical shapes can be made by working in the round. Within the written pattern, each row or round will be written out on its own line and have a designated row or round number (see the sample pattern on page 25).

ABBREVIATIONS AND OTHER TERMINOLOGY

To make pattern instructions easier to follow, as well as save time and space on the page, crochet stitch names are abbreviated rather than written out in full. Once you familiarize yourself with these abbreviations, pattern reading becomes a whole lot easier. See the chart on the right for most common crochet stitches and terms.

ABBREVIATIONS (US)	STITCHES AND TERMS (US)
alt	alternate
BLO	back loop only
beg	begin or beginning
ch(s)	chain(s)
ch-sp	chain space
dec	decrease
dc	double crochet
foll	follow(s) or following
FLO	front loop only
hdc	half double crochet
inc	increase
invdec	invisible decrease
mr	magic ring
pm	place marker
rem	remain or remaining
RS	right side
R	round or row
sc	single crochet
sk	skip
sl st	slip stitch
sp	space
st(s)	stitch(es)
tr	treble or triple crochet
tch	turning chain
WS	wrong side
yo	yarn over

Getting started 23

PARENTHESES, BRACKETS AND ASTERISKS

Crochet patterns use a few different symbols that indicate how to work the pattern. It is crucial to understand what each of the symbols below mean.

PARENTHESES (...)

Parentheses are often used to indicate a group of stitches that should be worked together into a single stitch of the row or round. For example:

(3 dc, ch 1, 3 dc) in next st
= 3 double crochet, chain 1 and then a further 3 double crochet all worked into the next stitch.

Parentheses may also be used to indicate the stitch count, so you know how many stitches you should have at the end of each row or round. For example:

R3: [Sc, inc] x6 (18)
= after working round 3, you should have 18 stitches at the end of the round.

SQUARE BRACKETS [...]

Square brackets and parentheses are often used interchangeably, however, most of the time, they're used to indicate instructions that should be repeated. For example:

[3 sc, inc] x6
= single crochet in next 3 stitches, increase in next stitch, then repeat that 6 times.

[Sc] x36
= 1 single crochet in each stitch, which is repeated 36 times.

2 sc, inc, [4 sc, inc] x5, 2 sc
= single crochet in next 2 stitches, increase in next stitch, [single crochet in next 4 stitches, increase in next st], which is repeated 5 times, single crochet in next 2 stitches.

ASTERISKS *...*

Asterisks are used to show a series of repeated instructions. For example:

Dc in next 3 sts; *ch 1, skip next st, dc in next st*, rep from * to * across the row
= repeat chain 1, skip next stitch, double crochet in next stitch until the end of the row.

***Sc, dc, hdc*; rep from * to * 5 times**
= work the stitches between the asterisks and then repeat them 5 times.

SAMPLE PATTERN
Below is a sample crochet pattern for a small sphere or ball that is worked in the round over 12 rounds. Here I walk you through the pattern, round by round and stitch by stitch, to explain how to interpret each of the lines of instruction.

R1: 6 sc in mr (6)
Make a magic ring and work 6 single crochet into the magic ring. You now have 6 stitches at the end of round 1.

R2: [Inc] x6 (12)
[Work an increase by making 2 single crochet in each stitch of the previous round], then work the instructions inside the square brackets a total of 6 times. You now have 12 stitches at the end of round 2.

R3: [Sc, inc] x6 (18)
[Work 1 single crochet in the first stitch of the previous round, then work an increase by making 2 single crochet in the next stitch], then work the instructions inside the square brackets a total of 6 times. You now have 18 stitches at the end of round 3.

R4: Sc, inc, [2 sc, inc] x5, sc (24)
Work 1 single crochet in the first stitch of the previous round, then work an increase by making 2 single crochet in the next stitch. Next, [work 1 single crochet in each of the next 2 stitches, then work an increase by making 2 single crochet in the next stitch] and work the instructions inside the square brackets a total of 5 times. Now, work 1 single crochet in the last stitch of the previous round. You now have 24 stitches by the end of round 4.

R5–9: [Sc] x24 (24) *5 rounds*
[Work 1 single crochet in each stitch of the previous round], then work the instructions inside the square brackets a total of 24 times to complete the round. Work this same round a total of 5 times. You still have 24 stitches at the end of rounds 5, 6, 7, 8 and 9.

R10: Sc, invdec, [2 sc, invdec] x5, sc (18)
Work 1 single crochet in the first stitch of the previous round, then work an invisible decrease. Next, [work 1 single crochet in each of the next 2 stitches, then work an invisible decrease] and work the instructions inside the square brackets a total of 5 times. Now, work 1 single crochet in the last stitch of the previous round. You now have 18 stitches at the end of round 10.

R11: [Sc, invdec] x6 (12)
[Work 1 single crochet in the first stitch of the previous round, then work an invisible decrease], then work the instructions inside the square brackets a total of 6 times. You now have 12 stitches at the end of round 11.

R12: [Invdec] x6 (6)
[Work an invisible decrease in the next stitch of the previous round] – work the instructions inside the square brackets a total of 6 times. You now have 6 stitches at the end of round 12.

Cut the working yarn, leaving a long tail and pull through the last stitch. Weave the yarn tail through the front loops only of the final round and gently pull to close the opening. Hide the yarn end inside the sphere.

LOOK OUT FOR SUBHEADINGS
While working through a pattern, be mindful of any subheadings – for example, head, body, arms, legs – as these indicate which part of the pattern you're working on. This is especially important in amigurumi patterns that are often worked in multiple parts.

GAUGE/TENSION
You will inevitably come across the term gauge, or tension, when exploring crochet patterns.

The gauge refers to the size of the stitches. It measures both the width and height of the stitches within a certain area of the crochet fabric. Since we don't all crochet in exactly the same way – some people will naturally hold the yarn tighter than others, especially when learning – differences in gauge can cause variations in the overall size of a finished piece. This is important when making items of a specific size, such as clothing, as you do need to match the designer's gauge to ensure the correct fit.

If a particular gauge must be achieved, the pattern will provide you with a measurement and the ideal number of stitches and rows or rounds within that measurement.

Using the yarn, hook size and stitch specified in the pattern, crochet a swatch at least 2 inches (5cm) larger than the given measurement for the swatch – usually 4 inches (10cm) – and count the number of stitches and rows within that area to see how your gauge compares to the designer's. This allows you to make any necessary adjustments, changing the hook size if necessary to achieve the recommended number of stitches.

For example:
Gauge/tension: 7 hdc and 5 rows = 4 inches (10cm) using 5mm (US H/8) hook, or the size required to achieve the correct gauge/tension.

This means that after you have made your swatch worked in half double crochet and have measured and marked out the centre 4-inch (10-cm) square, you should be able to count 7 half double crochet stitches across the width of the square and 5 rows over the height of the square. If you have more stitches and rows within the square than the pattern calls for, switch to a larger size hook and work another swatch. If you have fewer stitches and rows, switch to a smaller size hook and work another swatch.

Gauge is generally not such a key factor in amigurumi as it doesn't matter if the finished character turns out slightly bigger or smaller than the designer intended. The pattern will usually state as much. However, it's good to be aware of gauge as many beginners get confused by any size discrepancy despite using the same materials and having followed the pattern to the letter.

WRONG SIDE VS RIGHT SIDE OF AMIGURUMI

When you're not an experienced crocheter, it can be hard to identify the different stitches and it can be especially tricky to tell which is the right side and which is the wrong side of your piece. This is a common problem that beginners face. Luckily, since amigurumi is mainly worked in the round, there are obvious differences in appearance and texture between the two sides.

On the right side of the work, each single crochet stitch looks like a V. On the wrong side, however, they look like upside down Vs and you can see the horizontal bar of each stitch. The stitches on the wrong side also look bumpier and fuzzier, whereas the stitches on the right side appear tighter and more defined.

Another way to tell the right side from the wrong side is to make a note of which side your starting yarn tail is on. Your starting tail should always be on the inside of your piece and you should be crocheting in a clockwise direction.

As you're crocheting, you may find that your piece will naturally start curling towards you. A simple way to combat this is to curve the piece away from you as you crochet or flip it inside out after completing a few rounds (though this can be tricky for small pieces).

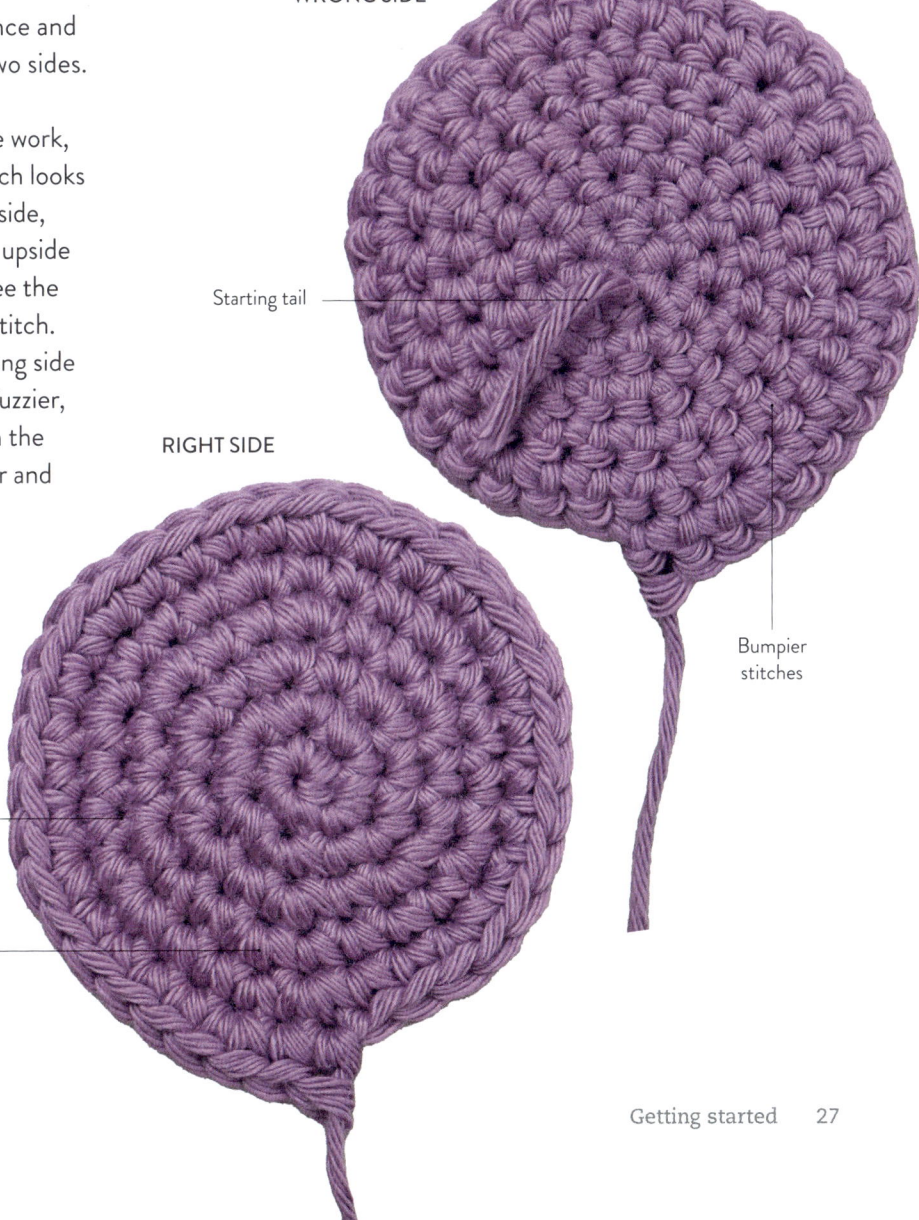

WRONG SIDE — Starting tail — Bumpier stitches

RIGHT SIDE — Stitches are tight and defined — A single crochet stictch looks like a V

STITCHES, TECHNIQUES & FINISHING

In this section, you'll learn all the basic stitches and techniques used in amigurumi, as well as how to add simple facial features which will really bring your amigurumi to life.

CROCHET BASICS

Before jumping straight into your first amigurumi project, I recommend taking some time to get comfortable with holding your hook and yarn by practising some of the basic stitches. It's important to note that there is no right or wrong way to crochet and it will take time to figure out what works best for you. Use the tips below as a starting point and remember, the more you practice, the easier it will become.

HOLDING YOUR HOOK

There are two main ways of holding a crochet hook.

Pencil grip
Hold the hook between your index finger and thumb, with your other fingers underneath to balance and control the hook. Grip the hook in the same way you would hold a pencil when writing.

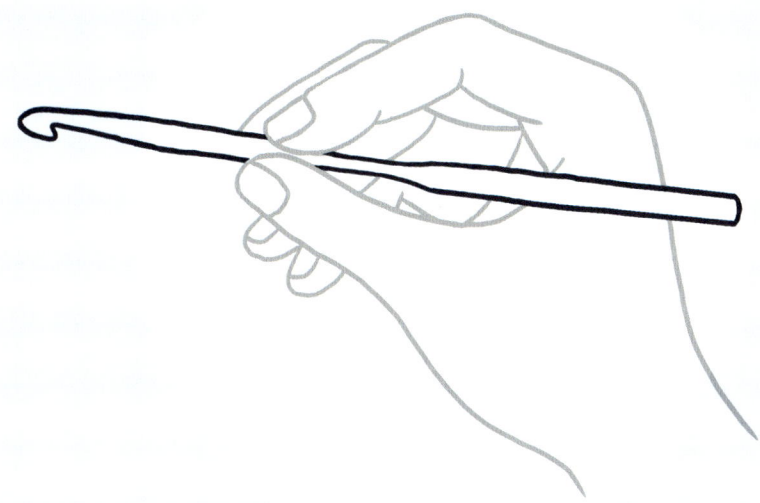

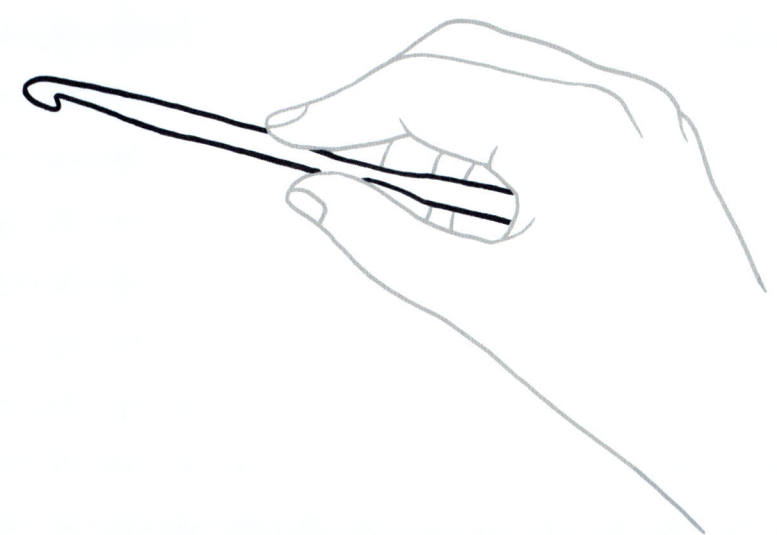

Knife grip
Hold the hook with your hand over the hook and your palm facing down, placing your thumb on one side and fingers on the other. Grip the hook in the same way you would hold a table knife when eating.

Whichever way you choose to hold your crochet hook, position your grip around 2 inches (5cm) down from the tip of the hook. Some hooks have a thumb rest to indicate where the hook should be held. If not, finding a good position to hold the hook will help to achieve regular stitches with an even gauge/tension.

CREATING A SLIP KNOT

Tying a slip knot is how you attach the working yarn to your crochet hook when working flat pieces in rows and is not counted as the first stitch on the hook.

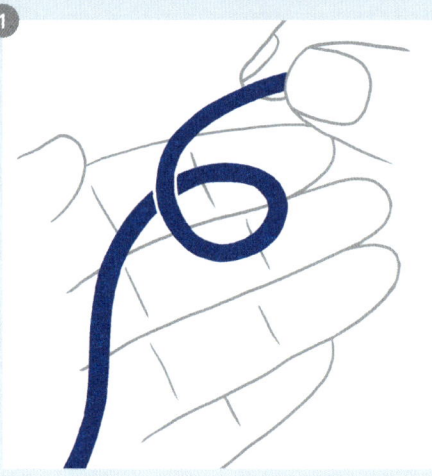

1 Make a loop with your yarn, making sure the working yarn (the side of the yarn attached to the ball) is on top and the tail end (the cut end) is underneath.

2 Insert your hook into the loop and use it to hook the working yarn. Pull the yarn back through the loop.

3 Pull both the tail and working ends of the yarn downwards at the same time to neaten up your slip knot. You will have a loop around the hook, with the knot underneath.

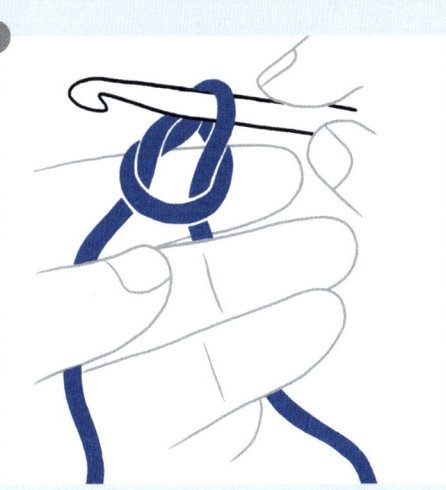

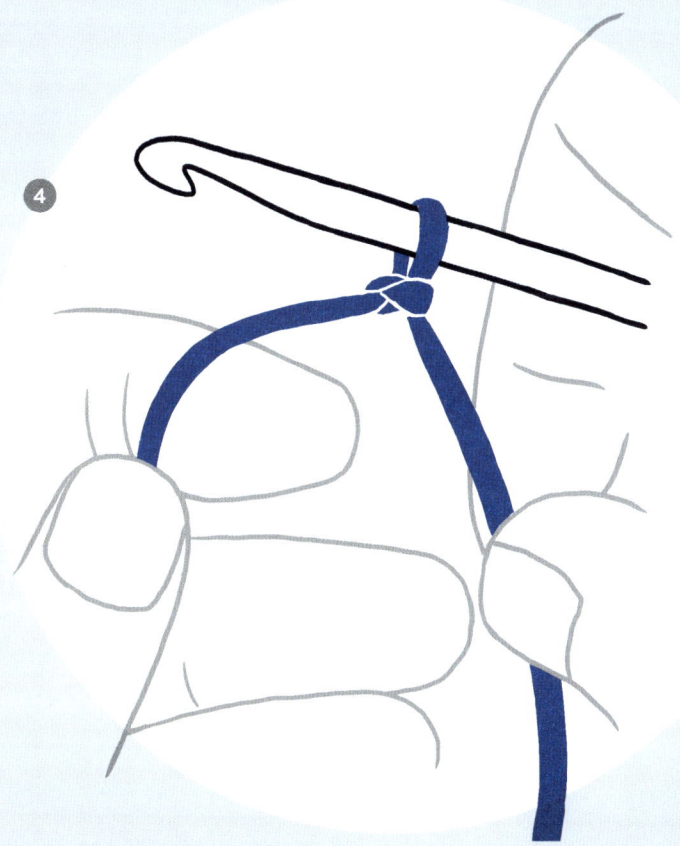

4 Pull the working yarn to tighten the slip knot. Be careful not to pull it too tight as you will struggle to crochet, but make sure it's not so loose that it falls off your hook.

HOLDING YOUR YARN

This is possibly the technique that requires the most practice because the way you hold your yarn controls the gauge/tension of your work. How tightly you hold the yarn as it flows through your fingers determines how loose or tight your crochet stitches and fabric will be. Having less tension on the yarn results in looser stitches and bigger gaps between stitches and vice versa. When it comes to amigurumi, it's important to maintain even tension throughout so as to create a firm fabric without any gaps.

There are a number of different ways of holding the yarn. To show you some of the different options, I've given the most common method as well as the method I prefer. You'll likely develop your own technique over time. The working yarn refers to the strand of yarn that's attached to the ball of yarn and the tail is the loose, cut end of the yarn.

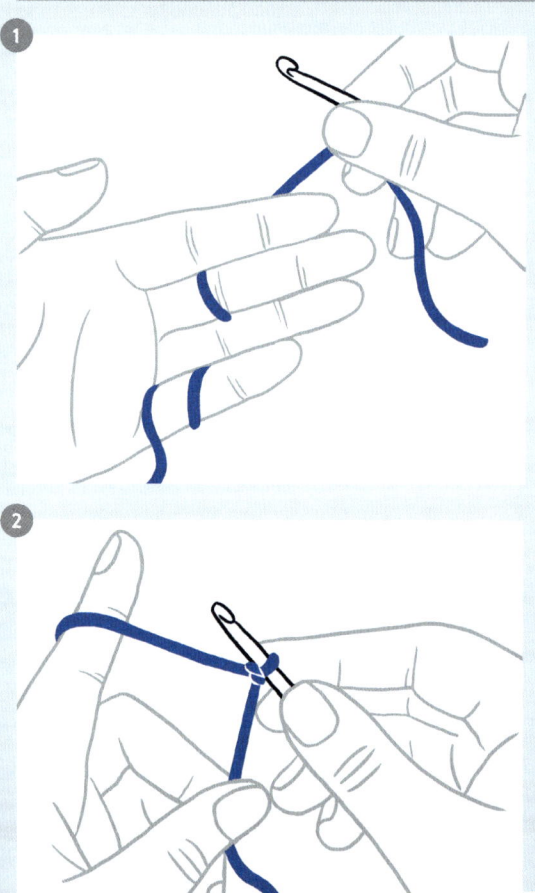

Common method
Start with a slip knot (see page 32) on your hook.

1 Wrap the working yarn around your pinky/little finger, over your ring finger, under your middle finger and over your pointer/index finger. Hold onto the tail end of yarn beneath the slip knot with your thumb and middle finger, with the working yarn resting over the top of your pointer/index finger.

2 Raise your pointer/index finger so you are ready to work the yarn between the hook and your pointer/index finger. To tighten or loosen the tension of the working yarn, move your pointer/index finger either towards or away from you.

34 Stitches, techniques & finishing

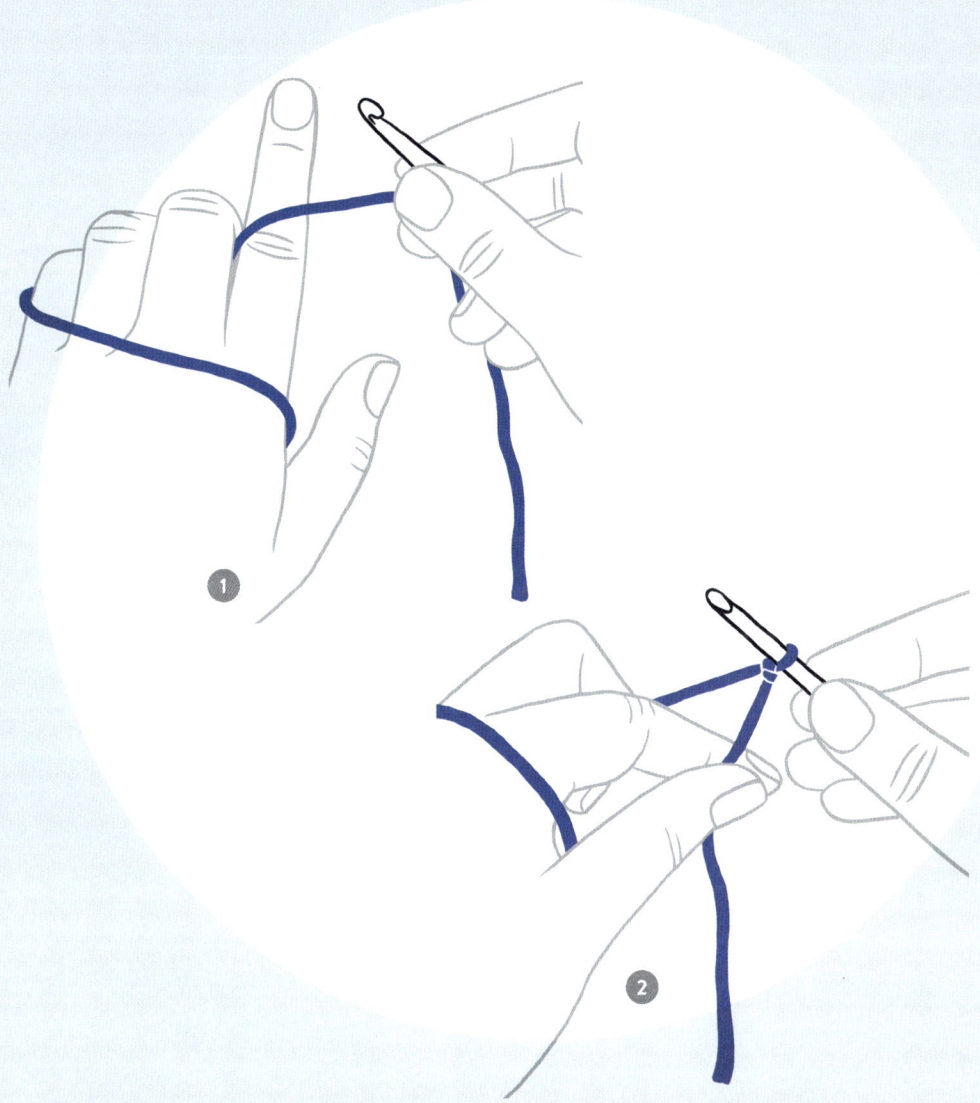

My method
Start with a slip knot (see page 32) on your hook.

1 Wrap the working yarn over the back of your hand at the base of your fingers, under the last three fingers of your hand and over your pointer/index finger.

2 Fold your last three fingers down so that the yarn glides through them and hold onto the tail end of yarn with your thumb and pointer/index finger.

Tensioning the yarn
It's necessary to apply some tension to the tail end of yarn to hold the slip knot in place. Depending on the method you're using to hold the yarn, use your free pointer/index or middle finger and thumb to pinch the yarn tail just below the hook.

Crochet basics

CROCHET STITCHES & OTHER TECHNIQUES

WORKING THE CHAIN STITCH (CH)

The chain stitch is the simplest of all crochet stitches. The first length of chain stitches is called the foundation chain (or a foundation ring when joined into a ring to work in rounds) and is the base from which you will work off for many crochet patterns, as the other stitches are made on top of these foundation chain stitches. In amigurumi, it's often used when creating accessories or embellishments, such as hair.

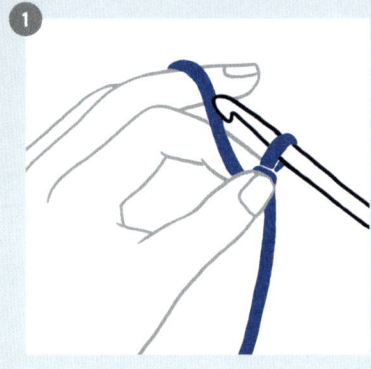

1 Start with a slip knot on your hook. Hold the tail end between your thumb and pointer/index finger or middle finger to keep the loop on your hook steady.

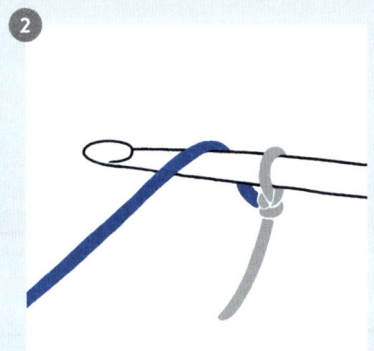

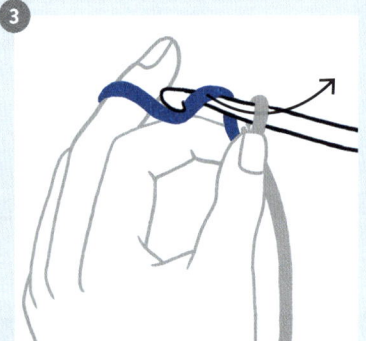

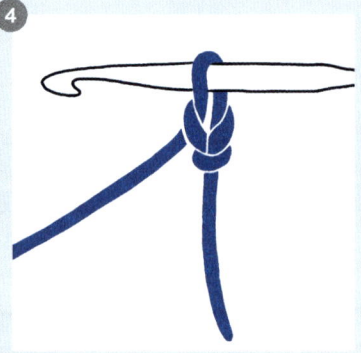

2 Bring the hook under and up behind the working yarn so that the yarn is lying across the hook from back to front. This is called yarn over (yo).

3 Grab the working yarn with the lip of the hook and rotate the tip of the hook towards you so that the working yarn remains caught in the lip. Draw the working yarn through the loop already on the hook. This makes a new loop on your hook. You've completed 1 chain stitch.

4 Repeat this process – yarning over and grabbing the yarn with the hook and drawing a loop through the one already on the hook – for each new stitch, moving your hand along the foundation chain as you work to maintain the tension. Crochet as many chain stitches as your pattern requires.

TIP

When you finish each stitch, slide the loop on your hook up onto the thicker part of the hook before moving on to the next stitch.

COUNTING CHAIN STITCHES

Counting stitches is an important part of the crochet process as a specific number of chains is needed to create the foundation row or ring. Having the wrong stitch count can throw off the whole pattern.

Always begin counting the chains from the base of the hook and work downwards. It's important to note that the loop on your hook does not count as a stitch. Count the number of Vs along the front of the foundation chain to determine how many chain stitches have been worked.

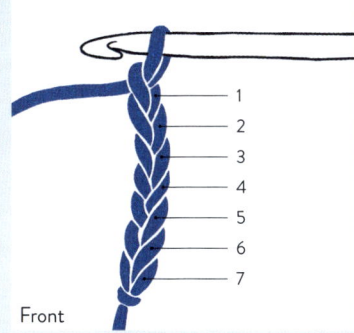
Front

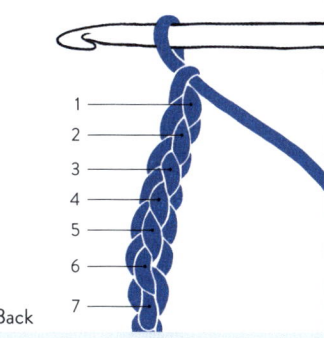
Back

Chain stitches have a front and a back. When the foundation chain of stitches is held in a vertical line, from the front they look like a stack of smooth V shapes. Each V is one chain. It's best to count chains from the front as the stitches are clearer.

The back of the foundation chain is made up of a series of bumps between each stitch. Whereas the front of the chain is smooth, the reverse side is textured. This is often referred to as the back bump of the chain. Depending on the pattern, you'll sometimes be instructed to work into the back of the chain.

WHERE TO INSERT YOUR CROCHET HOOK

When working into a foundation chain, as it is held horizontally with the Vs of the chain sitting in a line on top, the two sides of the V are known as the front loop (the one that's closest to you) and the back loop (the one that's furthest away). Most of the time, you'll insert your hook into the centre of the V and work with the back loop of the chain.

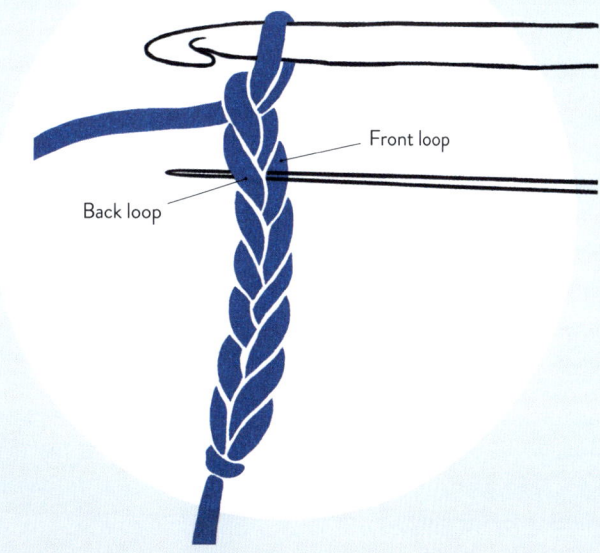

Crochet stitches & other techniques

WORKING SINGLE CROCHET (SC) INTO A FOUNDATION CHAIN

Amongst all the basic crochet stitches, single crochet is the shortest stitch. (The height of a crochet stitch is determined by the number of times the yarn is wrapped around the hook before it is drawn through the loop.) It's the primary stitch used for amigurumi as it creates the most tightly woven, stiff fabric and can be worked in either rows or rounds. Fortunately, it's also one of the easiest stitches to learn. Spend some time practising this key basic stitch and familiarizing yourself with holding and manipulating the hook and yarn.

> For this practice sample, start by making a slip knot (see page 32) and working a foundation chain (see page 36) of 15 chain stitches.

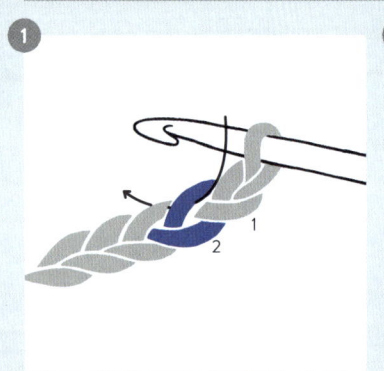
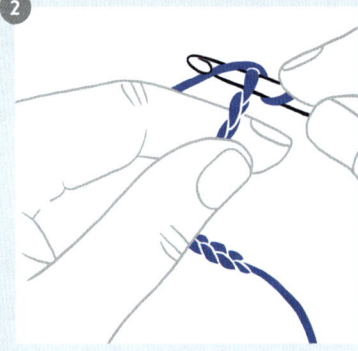
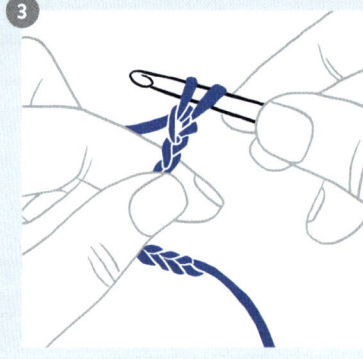

1 Remembering that the loop on the hook does not count, count along to the second chain from the hook. To work the first single crochet stitch, insert the tip of your hook through the centre of the second chain from the hook, passing it under only one strand of the chain (the back loop).

2 Bring the hook under and up behind the working yarn so that the yarn is lying across the hook from back to front.

3 Holding the foundation chain taut below the hook, grab the working yarn with the lip of the hook and draw the yarn through the first loop on the hook only (the second chain of the foundation chain) to make a new loop. There are now 2 loops on the hook (the new loop and the original active loop).

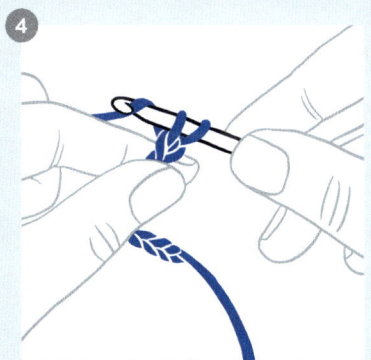 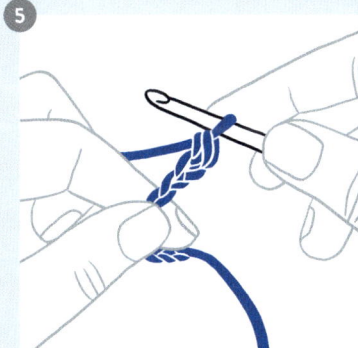

4 Bring your hook under and up behind the working yarn so that the yarn is lying across the hook from back to front.

5 Holding the foundation chain taut below the hook (moving along the foundation chain, if necessary), grab the working yarn with the lip of the hook and draw the yarn through both loops on the hook (the new loop and the original active loop). There is now 1 loop on the hook. You've completed one single crochet stitch.

6 Repeat this process for each new single crochet stitch, inserting the tip of the hook into the next chain along and moving your hand along the foundation chain as you work to maintain the tension. Crochet as many single crochet stitches as your pattern requires – here, work a single crochet into each of the remaining 13 chains for a total of 14 stitches.

WORKING SINGLE CROCHET (SC) IN ROWS

If you need to work further rows of single crochet, turn the piece so that the working yarn sits at the righthand edge ready to crochet back into the stitches of the previous row.

> **TIP**
> It can be helpful to count the number of stitches after each row and mark the first and last stitch of the row with a stitch marker as they can be easily missed.

1 Before beginning the new row, make one chain stitch for the turning chain (see page 36). This chain does not count as a stitch but is known as a turning chain and brings the sides of the work up to the same height as the single crochet stitches that follow (without a turning chain the piece will be uneven).

2 Look down on your work from above. You will see a series of Vs running along the top edge. To make the first stitch in a further row of single crochet, insert the tip of the hook under both strands of the first V (unless specified otherwise).

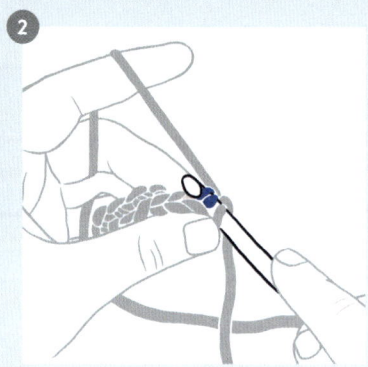

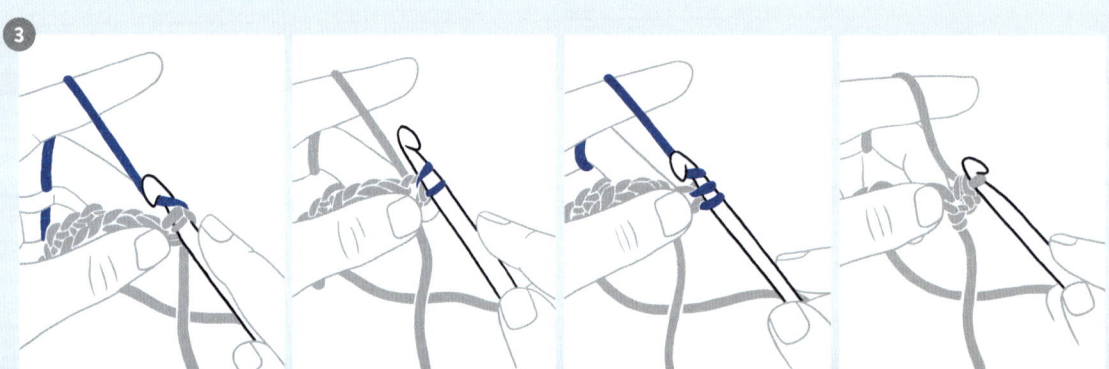

3 Complete the single crochet stitch as instructed above.

4 Continue along the row, working each single crochet stitch into both strands of the top of the single crochet stitch below. Make sure you don't skip the last stitch in the row. At the end of this row, turn the piece ready to start the next row.

5 Work all subsequent rows by working one chain (the turning chain) and completing single crochet stitches into each stitch of the previous row. Work as many rows as instructed in your crochet pattern or until the piece reaches your desired length.

YARN OVER VS YARN UNDER

As you progress in your crochet journey, you may come across a variation of single crochet that is primarily used in amigurumi. The difference is in the way in which you grab the working yarn when making a single crochet stitch. A traditional single crochet is formed by the yarn over method, where the yarn is placed over the hook before being drawn through the stitch. This is the most common way of working a single crochet and it is what I use for the projects throughout this book. When using the yarn under method, the yarn is grabbed when it's under the hook before being drawn through the stitch. The yarn under method creates a tighter stitch, which makes it a popular choice for amigurumi. However, using it may result in a smaller finished piece and a visual difference when following patterns that use the traditional yarn over method.

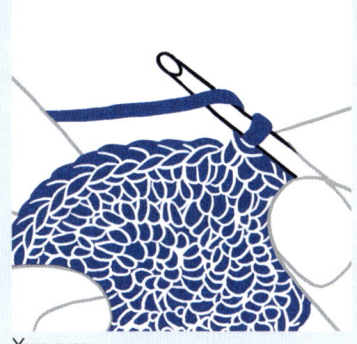
Yarn over

Once you've been making amigurumi for a while, whether you use the yarn over or the yarn under method, it becomes a matter of personal preference and what works best for your style of crochet. Just keep in mind that if you're making something where gauge/tension is important, you want to match the designer's stitches. Below is a chart to help you compare the differences.

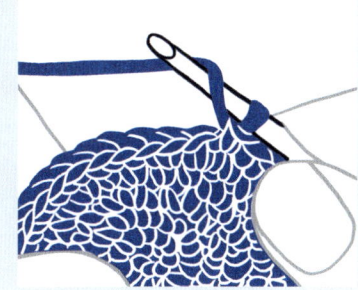
Yarn under

YARN OVER (YO)	YARN UNDER (YU)
Traditional	Non-traditional
Stitches are taller	Stitches are shorter
Uses slightly more yarn	Uses slightly less yarn
Stitches are slightly looser	Stitches are slightly tighter
Slants more	Slants less
Stitches look traditional	Stitches have an 'X' shape

TURNING CHAIN (TCH)

When working in rows of single crochet, the one chain stitch at the beginning of each row does not count as a stitch but rather it's the turning chain. The sole purpose of the turning chain is to bring your stitches up to the correct height of the new row. The length of the turning chain depends on the height of the stitch that comes after it.

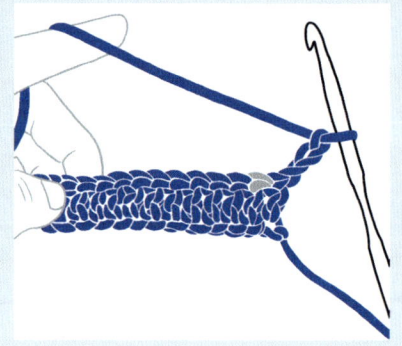

When working your first row of stitches into a foundation chain, you simply skip the required number of chains and make your first stitch in the next chain. The skipped chains act as the turning chain.

For example: dc in 4th ch = skip the first 3 chains just below the hook, then work a double crochet in the 4th chain from the hook.

Then when working the second row of stitches into the previous row, and any subsequent rows, you work the appropriate number of chains to make the correct length turning chain for the stitch of that row. Here (right) are the traditional turning chain lengths for the key basic crochet stitches.

The pattern will specify whether the turning chain counts as a stitch or not. This is important so you know where to place the first or last stitch of the row and whether or not to include it as part of your stitch count.

Some patterns will have you turn your work first and then chain and others will have you chain before turning. Whichever way you do it, it doesn't matter as long as you stay consistent throughout your piece and make sure to turn your work the same way each time.

TURNING CHAIN LENGTHS

single crochet	1 ch
half double crochet	2 ch
double crochet	3 ch
treble crochet	4 ch
double treble crochet	5 ch

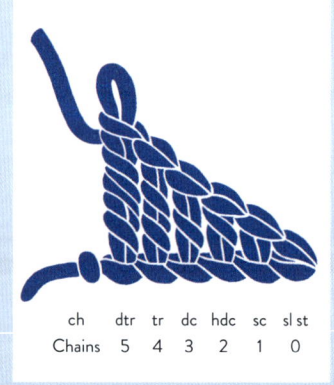

	ch	dtr	tr	dc	hdc	sc	sl st
Chains	5	4	3	2	1	0	

CROCHETING AROUND A FOUNDATION CHAIN

Some crochet patterns require you to crochet around a foundation chain to create a different shape, such as the sole of a foot or the base of a bag. To do this, work into the foundation chain in the usual way following the directions given above (see page 38) and passing the hook under only one strand of the chain (the back loop), until you reach the end of the foundation chain. Next, rotate the piece by 180 degrees and continue to work along the other side of the foundation chain into the unused strands of the chain (what was the front loop, but after the piece has been turned is now the back loop).

TIP
Working around the foundation chain in this way can stretch it, leaving large gaps down the centre. Try crocheting into both the front loop and the back bump of the chain for a neater finish.

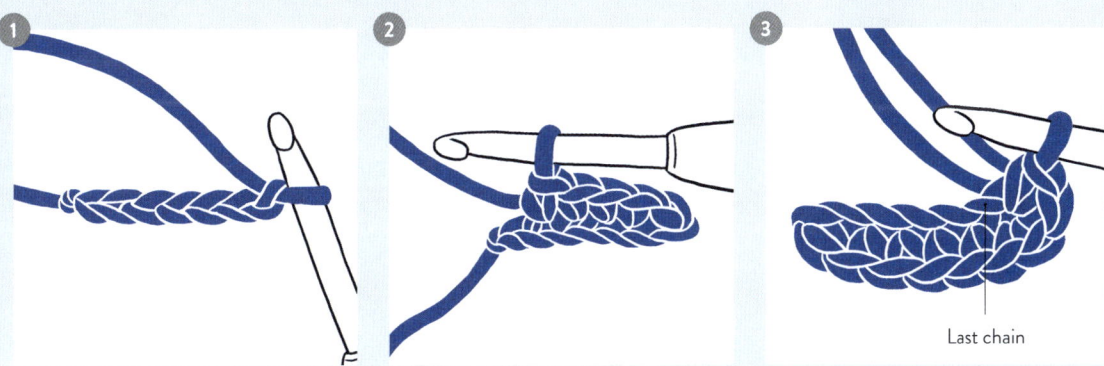

Last chain

1 For this practice sample, start by making a slip knot (see page 32) and working a foundation chain (see page 36) of 7 chain stitches.

2 Work one single crochet into the second chain from hook and then one single crochet into each of the next 4 chains of the foundation chain.

3 Work 4 single crochet all into the last chain of the foundation chain to take the working yarn around the end and over to the other, as yet unworked, side of the foundation chain.

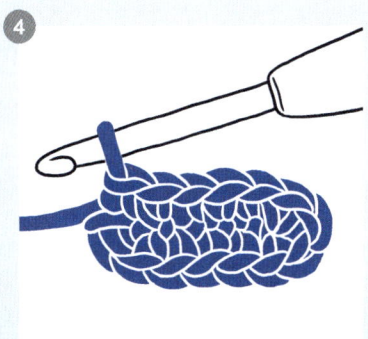

4 Work one single crochet into each of the next 5 chains of the unworked side of the foundation chain, which brings you back to the beginning of the round.

Crochet stitches & other techniques

HALF DOUBLE CROCHET (HDC)

The half double crochet is the next stitch up from single crochet in terms of height. It's the halfway point between the shorter single crochet and the taller double crochet. It creates a fabric that is still quite dense but more fluid than single crochet. It's worked in a similar way to single crochet except you make an extra yarn over at the start of each stitch.

For this practice sample, start by making a slip knot (see page 32) and working a foundation chain (see page 36) of 15 chain stitches.

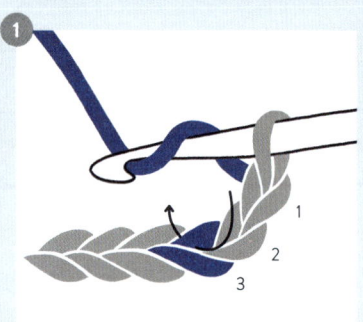
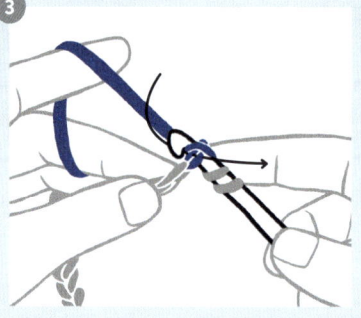
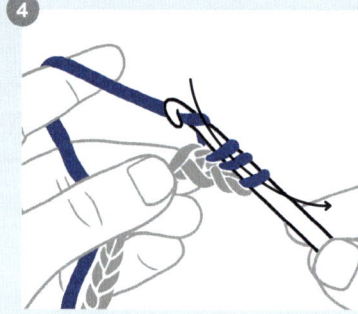

1 To work the first half double crochet stitch, bring the hook under and up behind the working yarn so that the yarn is lying across the hook from back to front. Remembering that the loop on the hook does not count, count along to the third chain from the hook. Insert the tip of your hook through the centre of the third chain from the hook, passing it under only one strand of the chain (the back loop).

2 Bring the hook under and up behind the working yarn again so that the yarn is lying across the hook from back to front and grab the working yarn with the lip of the hook.

3 Holding the foundation chain taut below the hook, draw the yarn through the first loop on the hook only (the third chain of the foundation chain) to make a new loop. There are now 3 loops on the hook (the new loop, the yarn over the hook and the original active loop).

4 Bring the hook under and up behind the working yarn so that the yarn is lying across the hook from back to front and grab the working yarn with the lip of the hook again.

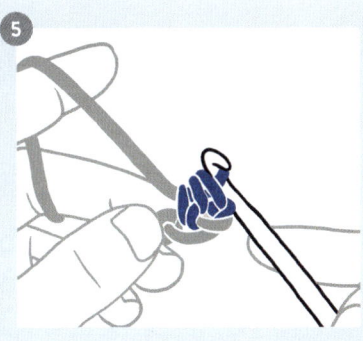

5 Holding the foundation chain taut below the hook (moving along the foundation chain, if necessary), draw the yarn through all 3 loops on the hook (the new loop, the yarn over the hook and the original active loop). There is now 1 loop on the hook. You've completed one half double crochet stitch.

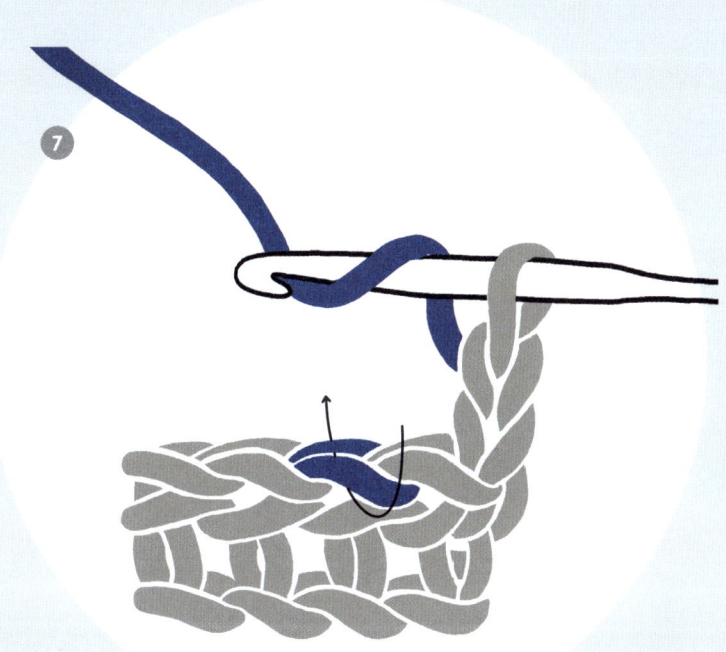

6 Repeat this process for each new half double crochet stitch, remembering to yarn over the hook before inserting the tip of the hook into the next chain along and moving your hand along the foundation chain as you work to maintain the tension. Crochet as many half double crochet stitches as your pattern requires – here, work a half double crochet into each of the remaining 12 chains for a total of 13 stitches.

7 If you need to work further rows of half double crochet, turn the piece so that the working yarn sits at the righthand edge ready to crochet back into the stitches of the previous row. Before beginning the new row, make 2 chain stitches for the turning chain which does not count as the first half double crochet stitch of this row. Yarn over and work a half double crochet stitch by inserting the tip of the hook under both strands of the top of the first stitch in the previous row. Continue along the row, working each half double crochet stitch into both strands of the top of the half double crochet stitch below.

8 Repeat for subsequent rows, working into each half double crochet stitch of the previous row.

Crochet stitches & other techniques

DOUBLE CROCHET (DC)

The double crochet stitch is twice the height of the single crochet stitch, which means it creates a more open, fluid fabric. That makes it a popular choice for garments, hats and other accessories. In amigurumi, you may come across double crochet being used for shaping or creating accessories. It's worked in a similar way to half double crochet, with an extra yarn over being made at the start of each stitch.

For this practice sample, start by making a slip knot (see page 32) and working a foundation chain (see page 36) of 15 chain stitches.

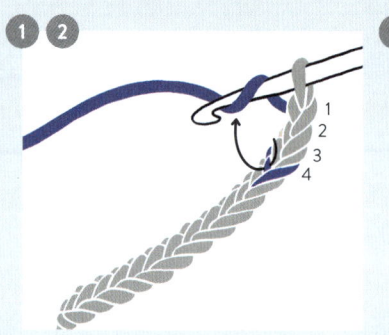 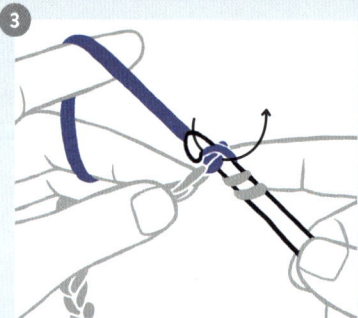 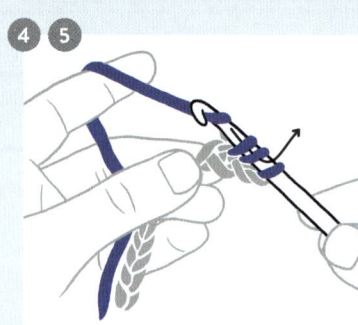

1 To work the first double crochet stitch, bring the hook under and up behind the working yarn so that the yarn is lying across the hook from back to front. Remembering that the loop on the hook does not count, count along to the fourth chain from the hook. Insert the tip of your hook through the centre of the fourth chain from the hook, passing it under only one strand of the chain (the back loop).

2 Bring the hook under and up behind the working yarn again so that the yarn is lying across the hook from back to front and grab the working yarn with the hook.

3 Holding the foundation chain taut below the hook, draw the yarn through the first loop on the hook only (the fourth chain of the foundation chain) to make a new loop. There are now 3 loops on the hook (the new loop, the yarn over the hook and the original active loop).

4 Bring the hook under and up behind the working yarn so that the yarn is lying across the hook from back to front and grab the working yarn with the lip of the hook again.

5 Holding the foundation chain taut below the hook (moving along the foundation chain, if necessary), draw the yarn through the first 2 loops on the hook (the new loop and the yarn over the hook). There are now 2 loops on the hook.

6 Bring the hook under and up behind the working yarn so that the yarn is lying across the hook from back to front and grab the working yarn with the lip of the hook again.

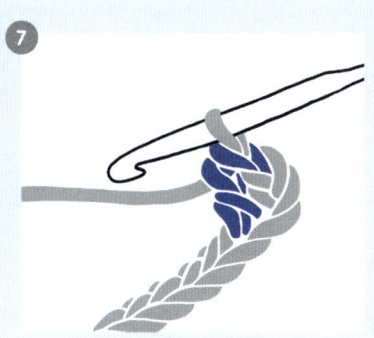

7 Holding the foundation chain taut, draw the yarn through both loops on your hook (the new loop and the original active loop). There is now 1 loop on the hook. You've completed one double crochet stitch.

8 Repeat this process for each new double crochet stitch, remembering to yarn over the hook before inserting the tip of the hook into the next chain along and moving your hand along the foundation chain as you work to maintain the tension. Crochet as many double crochet stitches as your pattern requires – here, work a double crochet into each of the remaining 11 chains for a total of 12 stitches.

9 If you need to work further rows of double crochet, turn the piece so that the working yarn sits at the righthand edge ready to crochet back into the stitches of the previous row.

Before beginning the new row, make 3 chain stitches for the turning chain which does not count as the first double crochet stitch of this row. Yarn over and work a double crochet stitch by inserting the tip of the hook under both strands of the top of the first stitch in the previous row. Continue along the row, working each double crochet stitch into both strands of the top of the double crochet stitch below.

10 Repeat for subsequent rows, working into each double crochet stitch of the previous row.

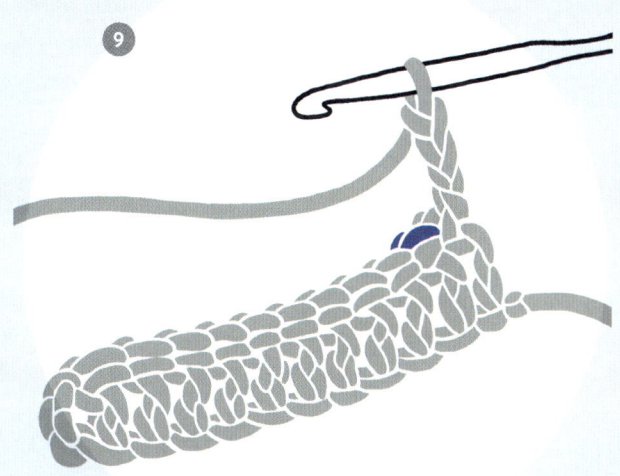

Crochet stitches & other techniques

TREBLE CROCHET (TR)

The treble crochet stitch (also referred to as the triple crochet stitch) is a tall stitch that creates a looser fabric. Because it is such an open stitch, it's not often used in amigurumi, but it's still considered one of the basic crochet stitches. It's worked in a similar way to double crochet, with two extra yarn overs being made at the start of each stitch.

> For this practice sample, start by making a slip knot (see page 32) and working a foundation chain (see page 36) of 15 chain stitches.

1 To work the first treble crochet stitch, bring the hook under and up behind the working yarn so that the yarn is lying across the hook from back to front. Repeat this movement again so there are two wraps of yarn around the hook. Remembering that the loop on the hook does not count, count along to the fifth chain from the hook. Insert the tip of your hook through the centre of the fifth chain from the hook, passing it under only one strand of the chain (the back loop).

2 Bring the hook under and up behind the working yarn again so that the yarn is lying across the hook from back to front and grab the working yarn with the lip of the hook.

48 Stitches, techniques & finishing

5 Holding the foundation chain taut below the hook (moving along the foundation chain, if necessary), draw the yarn through the first 2 loops on the hook (the new loop and one of the yarn overs). There are now 3 loops on the hook.

3 Holding the foundation chain taut below the hook, draw the yarn through the first loop on the hook only (the fifth chain of the foundation chain) to make a new loop. There are now 4 loops on the hook (the new loop, the two yarn overs and the original active loop).

4 Bring the hook under and up behind the working yarn so that the yarn is lying across the hook from back to front and grab the working yarn with the lip of the hook again.

6 Bring the hook under and up behind the working yarn so that the yarn is lying across the hook from back to front and grab the working yarn with the lip of the hook again.

7 Holding the foundation chain taut, draw the yarn through the first 2 loops on the hook (the new loop and the remaining yarn over). There are now 2 loops on the hook.

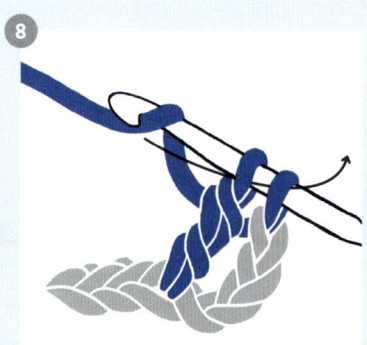

8 Bring the hook under and up behind the working yarn so that the yarn is lying across the hook from back to front and grab the working yarn with the lip of the hook again. Holding the foundation chain taut below the hook (moving along the foundation chain, if necessary), draw the yarn through both loops on the hook (the new loop and the original active loop).

9 There is now 1 loop on the hook. You've completed one treble crochet stitch.

10 Repeat this process for each new treble crochet stitch, remembering to yarn over twice before inserting the tip of the hook into the next chain along and moving your hand along the foundation chain as you work to maintain the tension. Crochet as many treble crochet stitches as your pattern requires – here, work a treble crochet into each of the remaining 10 chains for a total of 11 stitches.

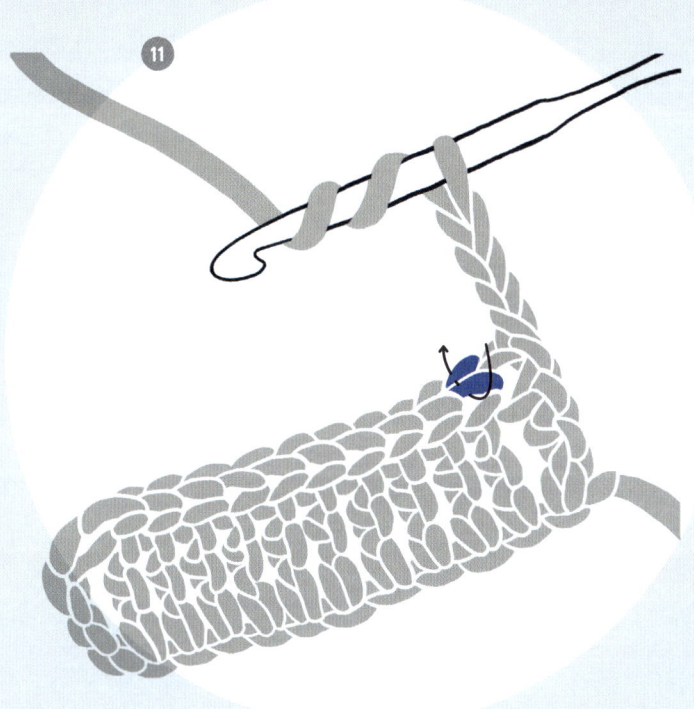

11 If you need to work further rows of treble crochet, turn the piece so that the working yarn sits at the righthand edge ready to crochet back into the stitches of the previous row. Before beginning the new row, make 4 chain stitches for the turning chain which does not count as the first treble crochet stitch of this row. Yarn over twice and work a treble crochet stitch by inserting the tip of the hook under both strands of the top of the first stitch in the previous row. Continue along the row, working each treble crochet stitch into both strands of the top of the treble crochet stitch below.

12 Repeat for subsequent rows, working into each treble crochet stitch of the previous row.

SLIP STITCH (SL ST)

Slip stitch is the shortest of the basic crochet stitches. While it's possible to work it into a fabric, slip stitch is most typically used to decrease the height of a round, join sections together or finish off a piece with a shallow edging as it doesn't add much height to your work.

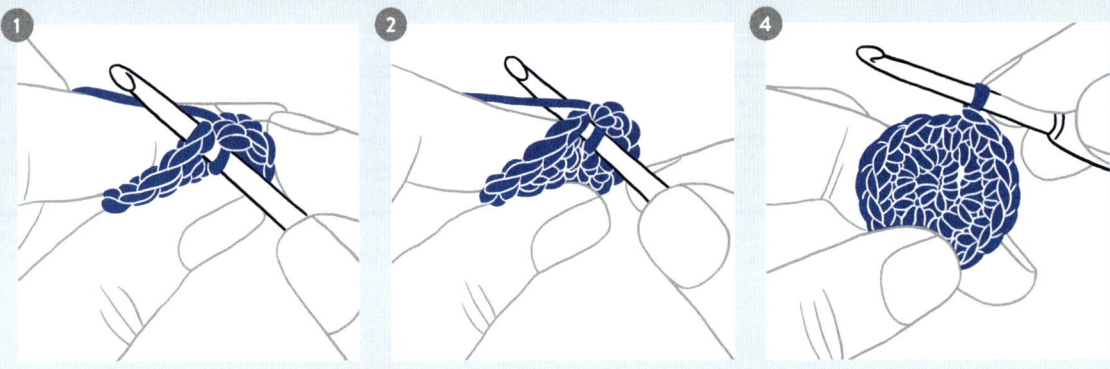

1 Insert the tip of your hook under both strands of the next stitch.

2 Bring the hook under and up behind the working yarn so that the yarn is lying across the hook from back to front and grab the working yarn with the lip of the hook.

3 Draw the yarn through the stitch on the hook.

4 There is now 1 loop on the hook. You've completed one slip stitch.

WORKING CROCHET IN ROUNDS

We've covered the basics of crocheting in rows (see page 40), so now let's take a look at crocheting in rounds. Rather than working forwards and backwards in horizontal rows, you make a central ring and work outwards from the ring in circles. Unlike working in rows where the piece is turned at the end of each row, when working in rounds, the right side of the work is facing you at all times. There are two different methods for working in the round:

- Joined rounds
- Continuous spiral

Most amigurumi are worked in the round using the continuous spiral method, however it's helpful to know the difference between the two methods and master the techniques.

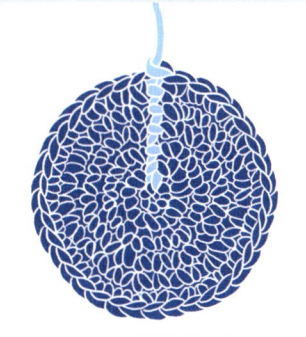 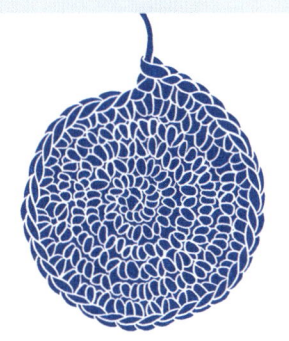

Joined rounds

When working in joined rounds, you crochet in the round without turning but each round begins with a chain stitch and, once all the stitches have been worked, it ends with a slip stitch into that chain to close the ring of stitches. The next round of stitches is worked on top of the previous round. There are some advantages to this method, especially when it comes to avoiding a step when changing colours, but the downside is the creation of a visible seam where the beginning and end of the rounds join.

The crochet pattern will specify if the beginning chain counts as a stitch or not within the round. This is important as it lets you know where to begin the round and where to join at the end of it. The joining slip stitch does not count as a stitch and should not be worked into.

Continuous spiral

When working in a continuous spiral, you crochet in the round without turning or joining. At the end of each round, you continue straight onto the next round with the first stitch of the new round being worked into the first stitch of the previous round, so you don't see where one round ends and another begins. This forms a spiral of stitches, which means the piece has no seam. While not having a seam may be considered an advantage, when changing colour in a round there will be a visible step at the point of the colour change. Also, since there is no visible beginning or end to a round, it's easy to lose track of which round you're working and so it's important to mark the first stitch of every round with a stitch marker so you know where you are.

COUNTING STITCHES AND ROUNDS

The number of stitches within a round can be counted either from the top of the round or from the side. In amigurumi, it's easiest to count the top of each stitch in the round as single crochet stitches are fairly short. Remember that the loop on your hook does not count as a stitch. When it comes to counting rounds, start by identifying the first round that was worked into the magic ring (see page 55). From here, count the rounds upwards from one side of the ring. I recommend using stitch markers when working in the round because it's not always easy to determine where a new round starts. Move the stitch marker each time you complete a round to easily identify the first stitch in that round and keep track of the number of rounds worked. Even if the number of stitches increases or decreases over the rounds, the first stitch will always be in the same place.

It can be helpful to keep a written note of where you are within a pattern, or print/photocopy the pattern so you can highlight instructions and tick off rounds as you go.

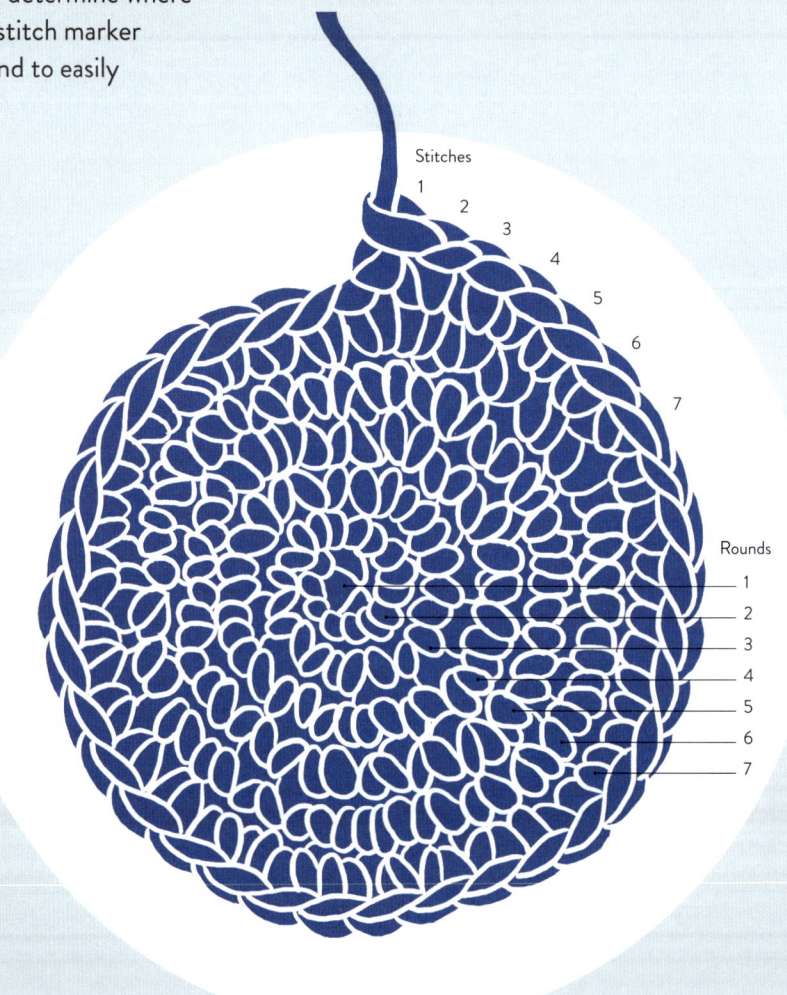

MAGIC RING (MR)

Most amigurumi patterns begin with a magic ring (also known as magic circle or magic loop). The magic ring is essentially an adjustable loop that your first round of stitches is crocheted into and, once you have the required number of stitches in the ring, you simply pull on the tail end of the yarn to cinch it closed. This creates a neat, tight centre in the middle of the piece with no visible hole. While it may seem fiddly at first, it's well worth taking the time and effort to master working a magic ring.

Making the magic ring
Unlike working a foundation chain, you do not make a slip knot but instead you create an adjustable loop of yarn.

1 Hold the tail end of the yarn in your right hand and the working yarn in your left hand. Leaving about 5 inches (13cm) of yarn at the tail end, make a loop with the working yarn sitting on top of the tail end.

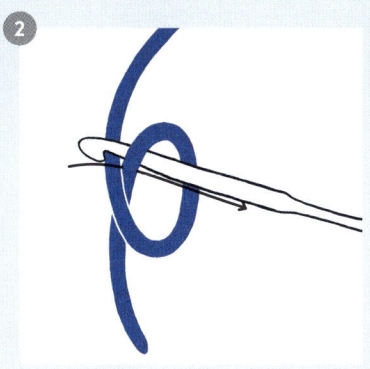
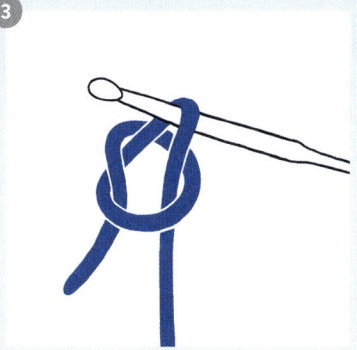
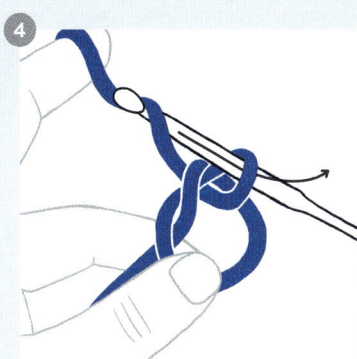

2 Holding the crochet hook in your right hand, insert it into the ring and catch the working yarn by placing the hook over the top of the strand.

3 Draw the working yarn through the ring to pull up a loop on the hook.

4 Now make a chain (see page 36) by yarning over and drawing the yarn through the loop on the hook. This chain does not count as a stitch.

Working into the magic ring
In this sample, we'll make 6 single crochet stitches into the magic ring. When working into the ring, make sure that the tail end of the yarn is sitting on the outside of the magic ring and not inside it. If it feels like your crochet stitches are twisting, gently pull on the tail end of the yarn to make the magic ring slightly smaller.

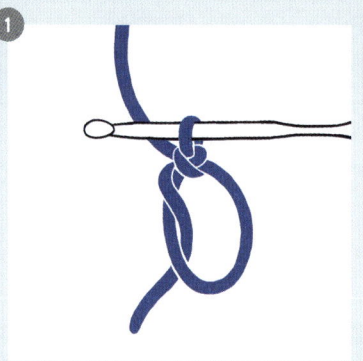

1 Insert the hook into the centre of the magic ring underneath both strands of yarn.

2 Yarn over and draw a loop through the magic ring. You now have 2 loops on the hook.

3 Yarn over and draw a new loop through both the loops on your hook. You now have 1 loop on the hook. You have worked one single crochet stitch.

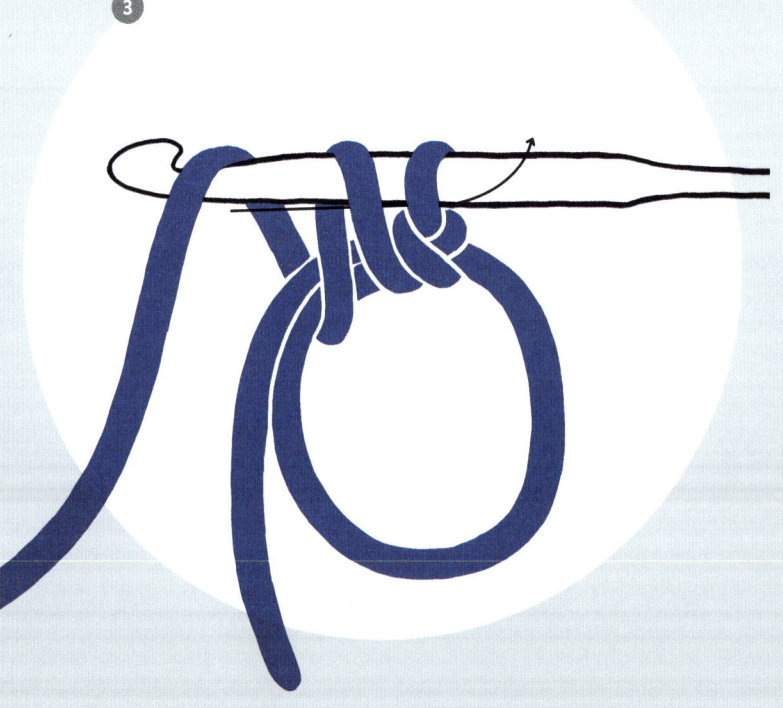

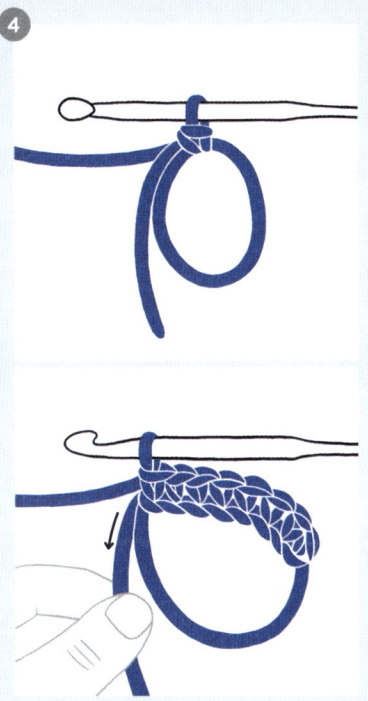

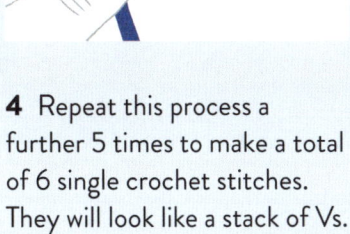

4 Repeat this process a further 5 times to make a total of 6 single crochet stitches. They will look like a stack of Vs.

5 To close the magic ring, hold the single crochet stitches in your right hand and gently pull the yarn tail with your left hand to tighten the ring. The magic ring will gradually close and the single crochet stiches will fan out into circle. Keep pulling the tail end until the hole at the centre of the magic ring is as small as possible.

TIP

If you find the crochet hook is getting in the way when tightening the magic ring, make the active loop on the hook larger and slide the hook out before pulling the ring closed. Slide the hook back into the active loop to continue.

Securing the magic ring
If the yarn you're using is particularly slippery or you're worried about the magic ring loosening or coming undone, you can secure it on the inside of your piece with a small knot. It's easiest to do this after completing a few rounds.

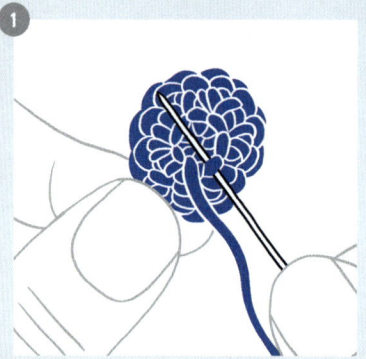

1 Thread the tail end of the yarn onto a yarn needle. Insert the needle through the back of the crochet stitch closest to where the tail end emerges.

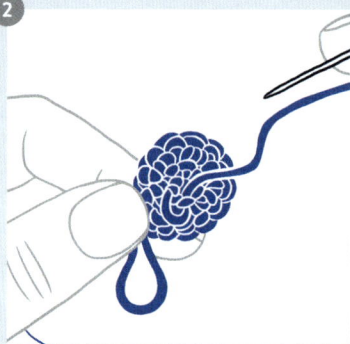

2 Pull the threaded yarn part of the way through the stitch but leave a small loop.

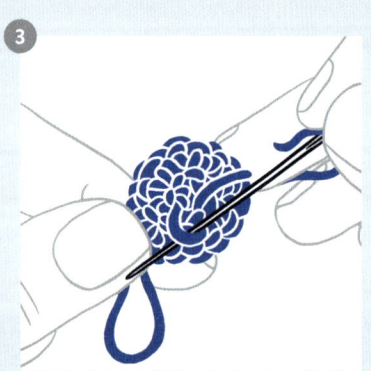

3 Pass the needle through the small loop, then pull it up to tighten and secure the tail end.

58   Stitches, techniques & finishing

WORKING AN INCREASE (INC)

An increase is when two or more crochet stitches are made into the same stitch of the previous row or round. By working an increase you're adding extra stitches to make the row or round wider, which makes it possible to create the spherical shapes that are often used in amigurumi.

1 At the point of the increase, work the first crochet stitch into the correct stitch of the row or round in the usual way.

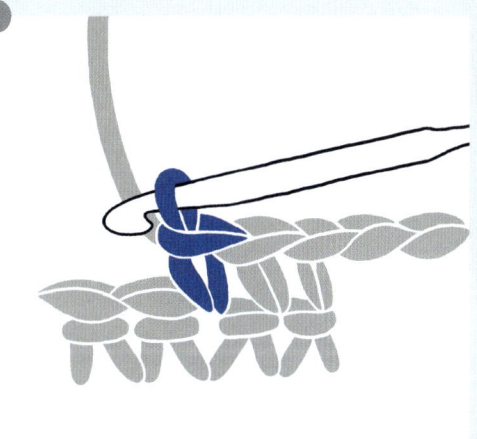

2 Insert the hook once more into the same stitch of the row or round and work a second stitch in the usual way next to the first. This completes the increase by one stitch. If the pattern instructs you to make an increase of more than one stitch, then work further crochet stitches in the same stitch as needed.

DECREASE (DEC OR SC2TOG)

A decrease is the opposite of an increase: two or more crochet stitches are worked together to reduce the stitch count and make the row or round narrower. This enables you to taper off crochet shapes. While most of the projects in this book are made using the invisible decrease method (see right), you may come across patterns in which a standard decrease is called for. A standard decrease is generally used on a project where both sides of the piece are visible, so anything worked in turned rows.

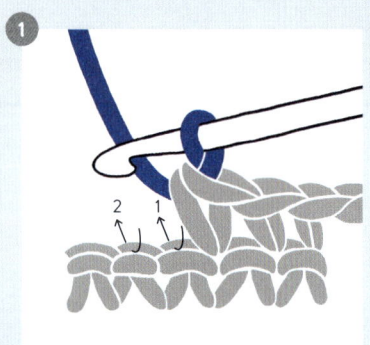

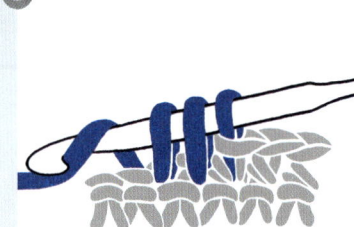

2 Yarn over and draw the yarn through all 3 loops on the hook.

3 This completes the decrease by one stitch.

1 Insert the hook under both the front and back strands of the next stitch. Yarn over and draw the yarn through both strands to make a new loop. You now have 2 loops on the hook. Insert the hook under both front and back strands of the next stitch. Yarn over and draw the yarn through both strands to make a new loop. You now have 3 loops on the hook.

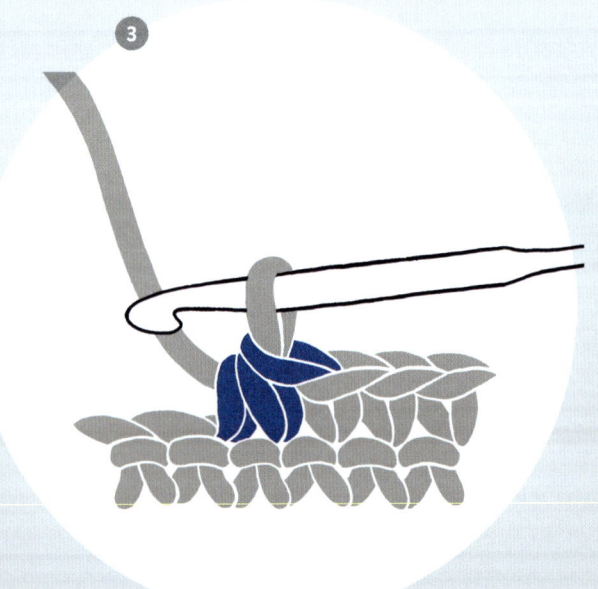

60   Stitches, techniques & finishing

INVISIBLE DECREASE (INVDEC)

The invisible decrease is the preferred way to decrease in amigurumi as it reduces any gaps between stitches. The invisible decrease is worked over two stitches.

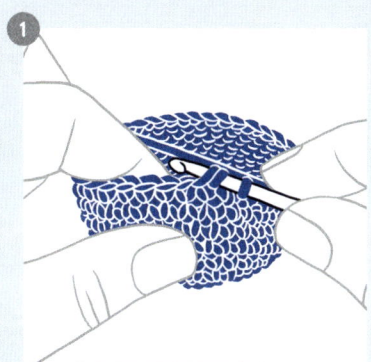

1 Insert the hook into the front loops only of the next 2 stitches. You now have 3 loops on the hook.

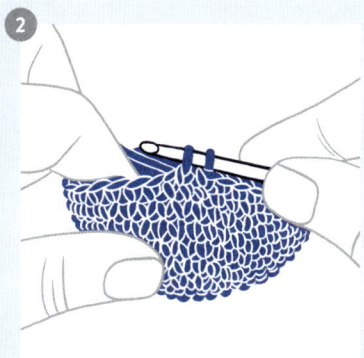

2 Yarn over and draw the yarn through the first 2 loops on the hook. You now have 2 loops on the hook.

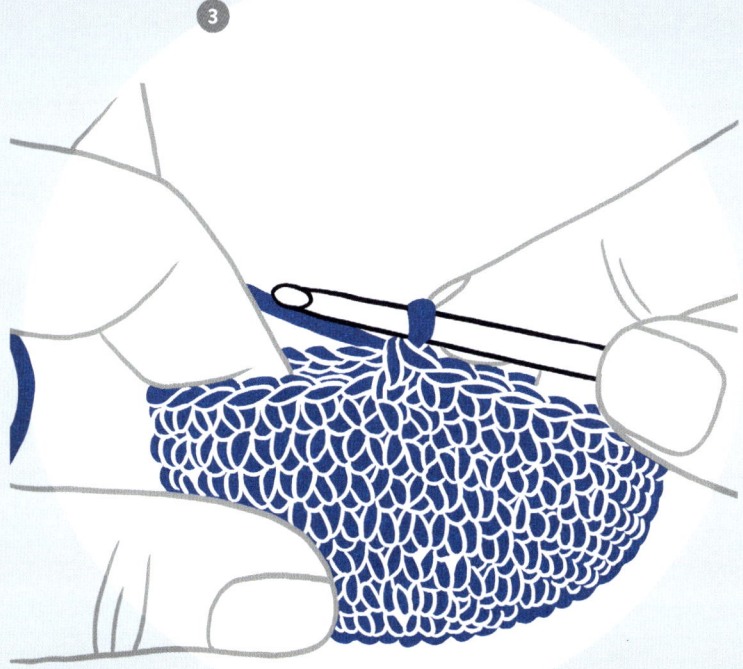

3 Yarn over and draw the yarn through the remaining 2 loops on the hook. This completes the invisible decrease by one stitch.

Crochet stitches & other techniques

ALTERNATING INCREASES AND DECREASES

One of the most common questions asked by beginners is: why do my flat circles look like hexagons? This is caused by stacking all of the increases in each round on top of one another, which is how a lot of crochet patterns are written. The shape does even out and become rounder when stuffing is added, however, if it really bothers you, there's a simple way to adjust any crochet pattern to replace stacked increases with alternating increases. As indicated in bold in the table (right), simply halve the first group of stitches of each even increase round from round 4 onwards. This spaces out the increases so that they are less noticeable overall and you end up with a perfect circle.

The same method can be applied when decreasing.

All the patterns in this book are written with alternating increases and decreases to ensure a clean finish every time.

STACKED INCREASES	ALTERNATING INCREASES
R1: 6 sc in mr (6)	R1: 6 sc in mr (6)
R2: [Inc] x6 (12)	R2: [Inc] x6 (12)
R3: [1 sc, inc] x6 (18)	R3: [1 sc, inc] x6 (18)
R4: [2 sc, inc] x6 (24)	**R4: 1 sc**, inc, [2 sc, inc] x5, **sc** (24)
R5: [3 sc, inc] x6 (30)	R5: [3 sc, inc] x6 (30)
R6: [4 sc, inc] x6 (36)	**R6: 2 sc**, inc, [4 sc, inc] x5, **2 sc** (36)
R7: [5 sc, inc] x6 (42)	R7: [5 sc, inc] x6 (42)
R8: [6 sc, inc] x6 (48)	**R8: 3 sc**, inc, [6 sc, inc] x5, **3 sc** (48)

STACKED DECREASES	ALTERNATING DECREASES
R9: [6 sc, dec] x6 (42)	**R9: 3 sc**, dec, [6 sc, dec] x5, **3 sc** (42)
R10: [5 sc, dec] x6 (36)	R10: [5 sc, dec] x6 (36)
R11: [4 sc, dec] x6 (30)	**R11: 2 sc**, dec, [4 sc, dec] x5, **2 sc** (30)
R12: [3 sc, dec] x6 (24)	R12: [3 sc, dec] x6 (24)
R13: [2 sc, dec] x6 (18)	**R13: 1 sc**, dec, [2 sc, dec] x5, **sc** (18)
R14: [1 sc, dec] x6 (12)	R14: [1 sc, dec] x6 (12)
R15: [Dec] x6 (6)	R15: [Dec] x6 (6)

CHANGING COLOURS

When crocheting amigurumi, changing yarn colour takes place in the last stitch immediately before the new colour is needed. You can also use the same technique to introduce a fresh ball of yarn in the same colour when the existing ball runs out.

NOTE

When working in a continuous spiral, you may notice a step where the colour change takes place. This is perfectly normal and, while there are ways to minimize the effects of the colour change, I don't think any of them are entirely invisible. Some amigurumi patterns will hide any colour changes by making sure that they happen in the least obvious place, such as at the back or the inside of a limb.

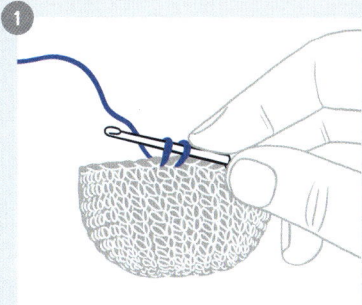

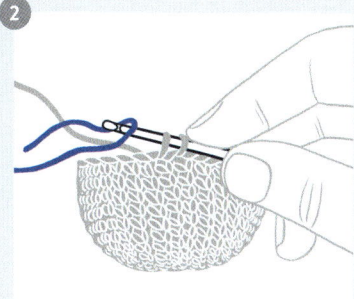

1 Work all the way along the round, stopping when there is just one stitch left in the round. Crochet the next stitch in the usual way until the final stage when you have 2 loops left on the hook.

2 Let the working yarn in the existing colour drop to the back of the work and drape the yarn in the new colour over your hook, leaving a yarn tail of approximately 4 inches (10cm).

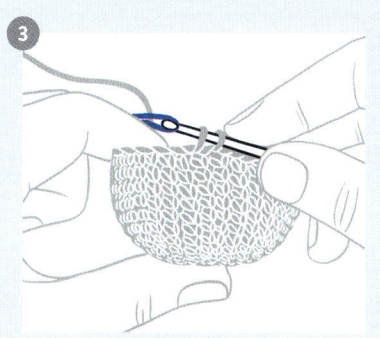

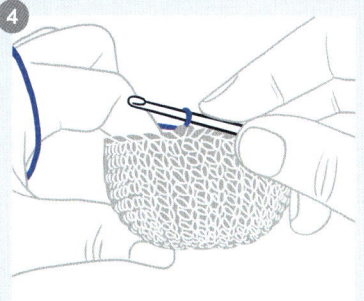

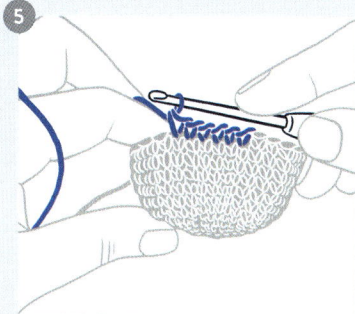

3 Grab the new colour yarn with the hook and draw it through the 2 loops on the hook to complete the stitch and make the colour change.

4 Gently tug the yarn tails to tighten the last stitch of the round, then continue crocheting with the new colour yarn.

5 If the old colour yarn is no longer needed, cut that yarn and secure it by knotting the two loose ends together on the inside of the piece.

WORKING INTO THE FRONT LOOP ONLY OR BACK LOOP ONLY

While crochet stitches are generally worked under both strands of the existing stitch of the row or round, there will be times when you'll be required to work through just the front loop (FLO) or back loop (BLO). Working into one or the other of these different loops can change the overall look and shape of a piece. By working under only one loop, a ridge is created by the unused loops of the stitches. This can be done for a purely decorative reason or these unused loops can be used to crochet back into later for adding additional details.

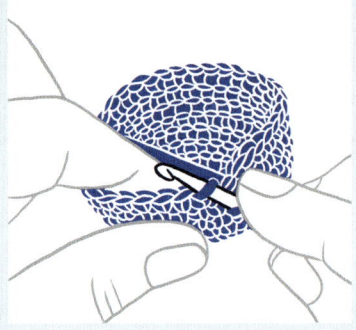

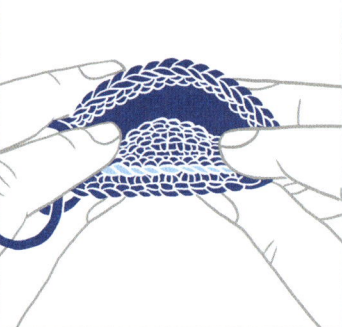

Front loop only (FLO)
To crochet into the front loop only, insert the tip of your hook into the strand of the stitch that is closest to you.

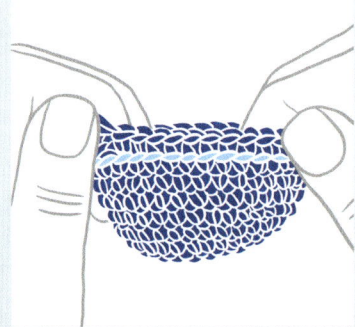

Back loop only (BLO)
To crochet into the back loop only, insert the hook into the strand of the stitch that is furthest from you.

JOINING YARN IN UNWORKED FRONT LOOPS

In order to add additional details to an amigurumi character, such as a skirt, collar or decorative trim, you may need to join new yarn to a round of leftover unused front loops.

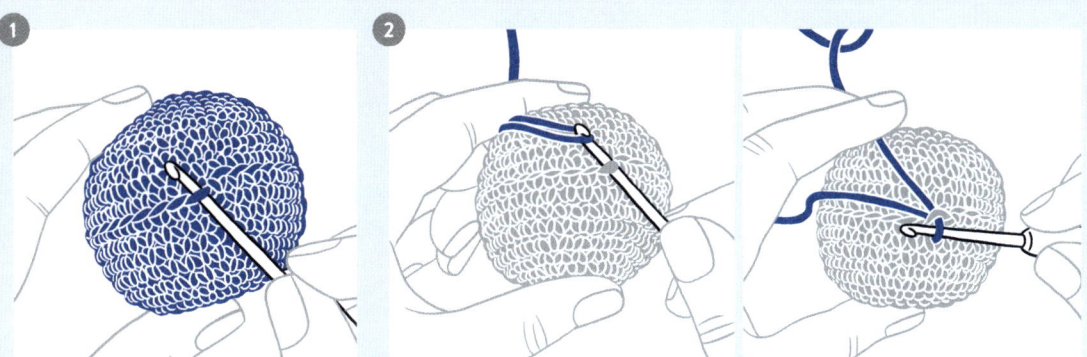

1 Holding the piece upside down, insert your hook into the first leftover unused front loop on the right side of the work.

2 Leaving a yarn tail of approximately 4 inches (10cm), drape the working yarn over your crochet hook, then grab the yarn with the hook and draw it through the front loop to pull up a loop on the hook.

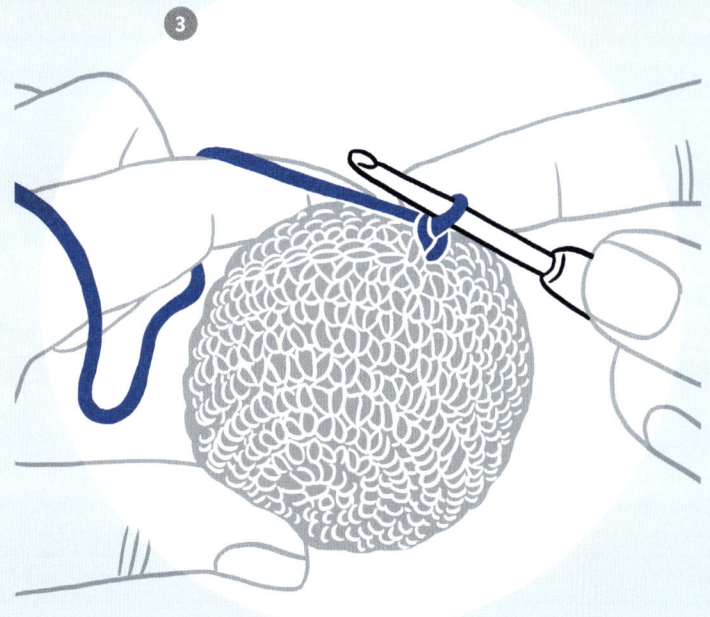

3 Now make a chain (see page 36) by yarning over and drawing the yarn through the loop on the hook. This chain does not count as a stitch.

Crochet stitches & other techniques 65

CROCHETING AN AMIGURUMI PIECE CLOSED

When finishing off a cylindrical piece of crochet for amigurumi, such as an arm, ear or wing, crocheting the piece closed gives a clean finished edge. This makes it easier when sewing the closed piece to another piece. It requires you to bring the two sides of the open cylinder together and work through both the front and back layers of the piece to close the opening.

The practice sample uses single crochet, but the technique is the same no matter what crochet stitch is being worked.

1 Making sure that your hook with the active loop is positioned on the far righthand edge, pinch the open end of the cylinder closed, lining up the stitches on the front layer with the stitches on the back layer.

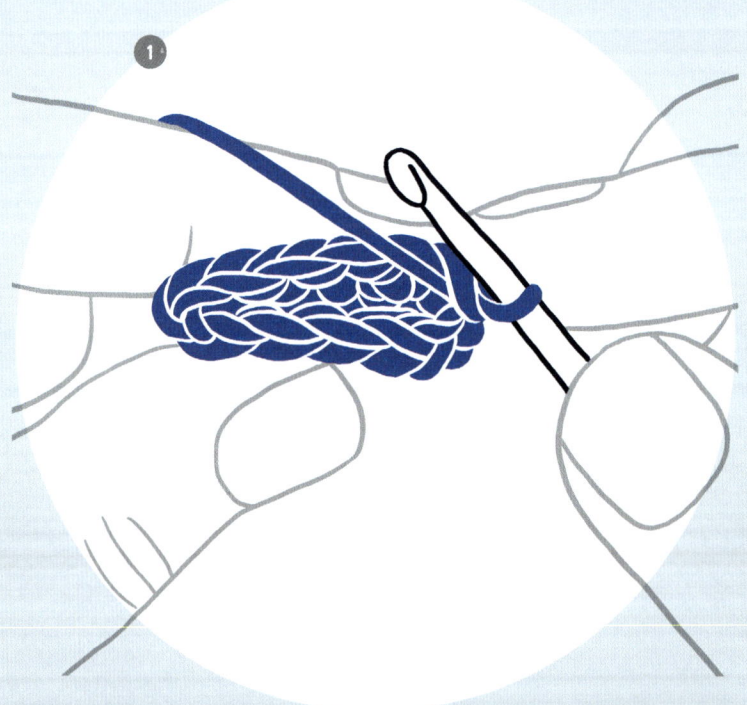

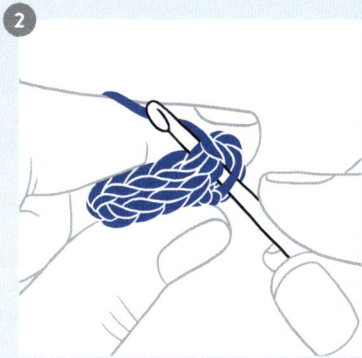 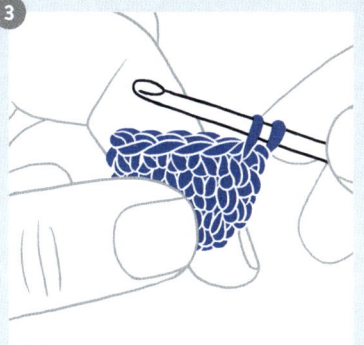 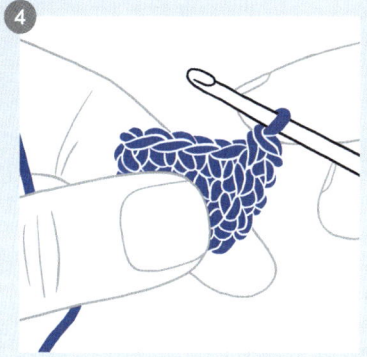

2 Insert the hook under both strands of the first stitch on the front layer and the corresponding stitch behind it on the back layer.

3 Yarn over and draw the yarn through both the front and back layers to make a new loop. There are now 2 loops on the hook (the new loop and the active loop).

4 Yarn over and draw the yarn through both loops on the hook to complete the first single crochet stitch.

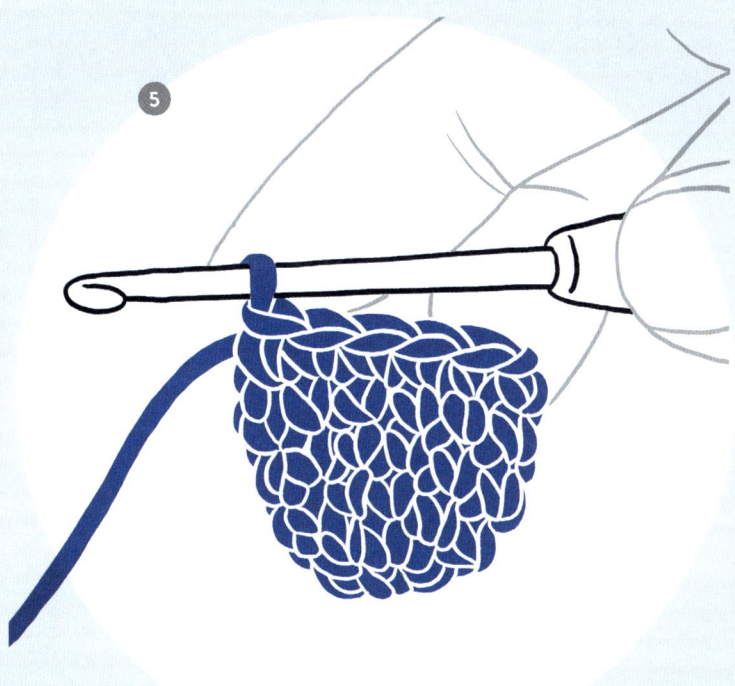

5 Repeat the process across the front and back layers until the opening is closed.

Crochet stitches & other techniques

CROCHETING AMIGURUMI PIECES TOGETHER

This technique allows you to join multiple pieces together into one continuous round. This is a great method for joining legs to create a one-piece body or for adding fingers to a hand and toes to a foot. Amigurumi pieces can be joined right next to each other or with a chain stitch separating them. Using stitch markers to keep track of your stitches is really helpful here, as well as counting the stitches both before and after to make sure you have the correct number of stitches before continuing with the pattern.

Joining two amigurumi pieces right next to each other
To work this method, you need two completed amigurumi pieces worked in the round, the first one that has been fastened off with a 4-inch (10-cm) yarn tail and the second one that is still attached to the working yarn. The two pieces are joined with no extra stitches being worked in between them.

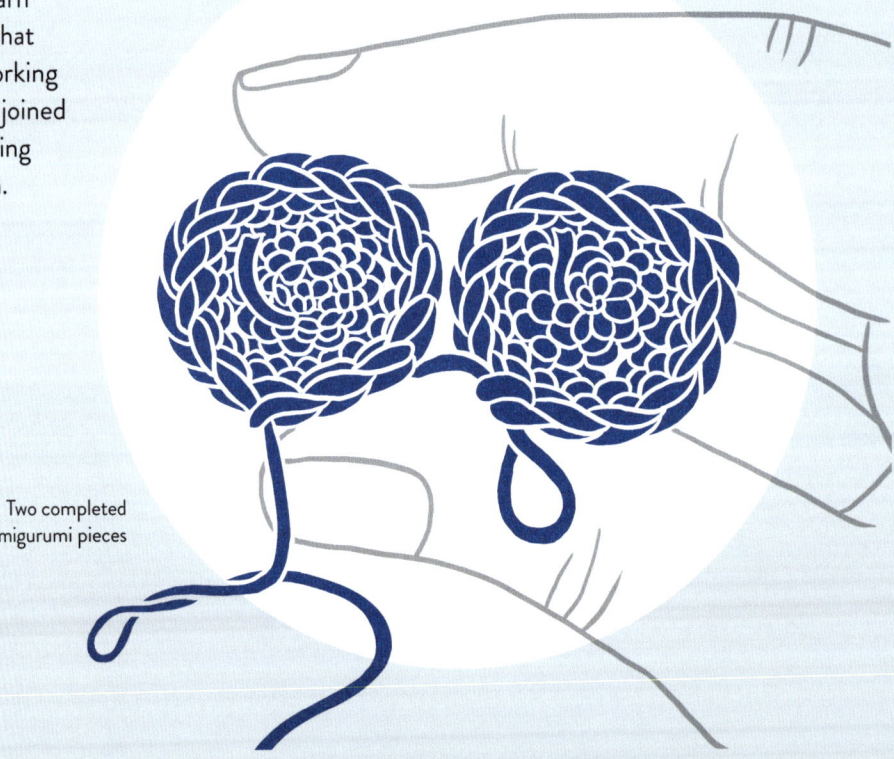

Two completed amigurumi pieces

68   Stitches, techniques & finishing

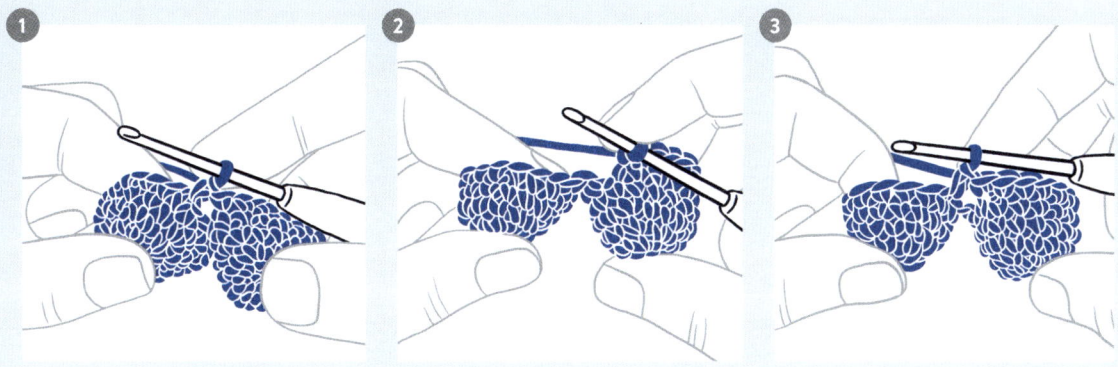

1 With the working yarn from the second piece on your hook, take the first fastened-off piece and insert the hook into the first stitch of the last round. Work a single crochet stitch to join the two pieces together.

2 Work a single crochet stitch into each of the remaining stitches of the first fastened-off piece to bring you back around to the second piece.

3 Insert the hook into the first stitch of the last round of the second piece. Work a single crochet stitch.

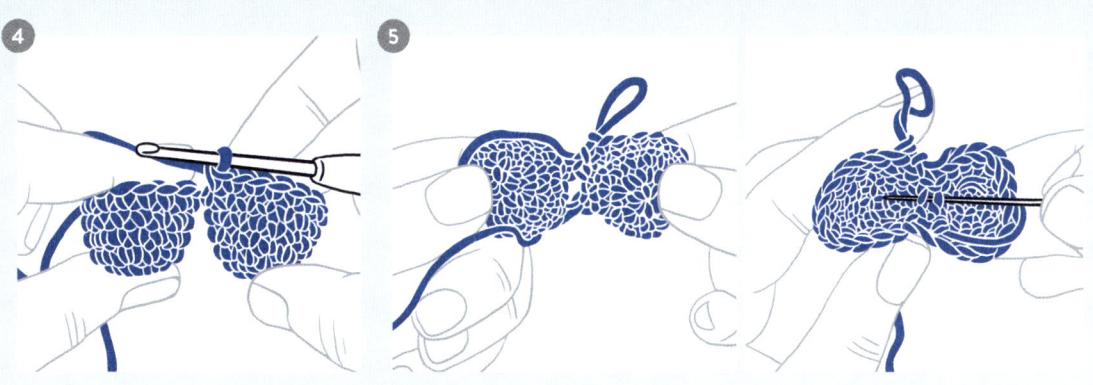

4 Work a single crochet stitch into each of the remaining stitches of the second piece until you reach the end of the round.

5 There will be a small gap between the two joined pieces, using the yarn tail from the first piece, make a couple of stitches through the centre to close the gap. Continue to crochet in a spiral as instructed by the pattern.

Joining two amigurumi pieces with a chain between them
To work this method, you need two completed amigurumi pieces worked in the round, the first one that has been fastened off and the second one that is still attached to the working yarn. In this example, three chain stitches are worked between the two pieces.

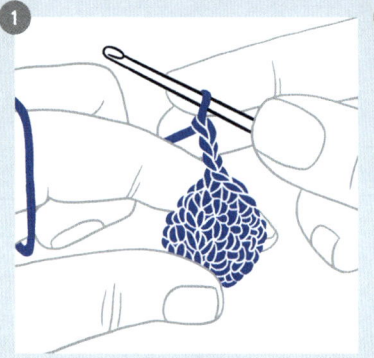

1 With the working yarn from the second piece on your hook, work 3 chain stitches. Take the first fastened-off piece and insert the hook into the first stitch of the last round. Work a single crochet stitch to join the two pieces together.

2 Work a single crochet stitch into each of the remaining stitches of the first fastened-off piece to bring you back around to the 3 chain stitches.

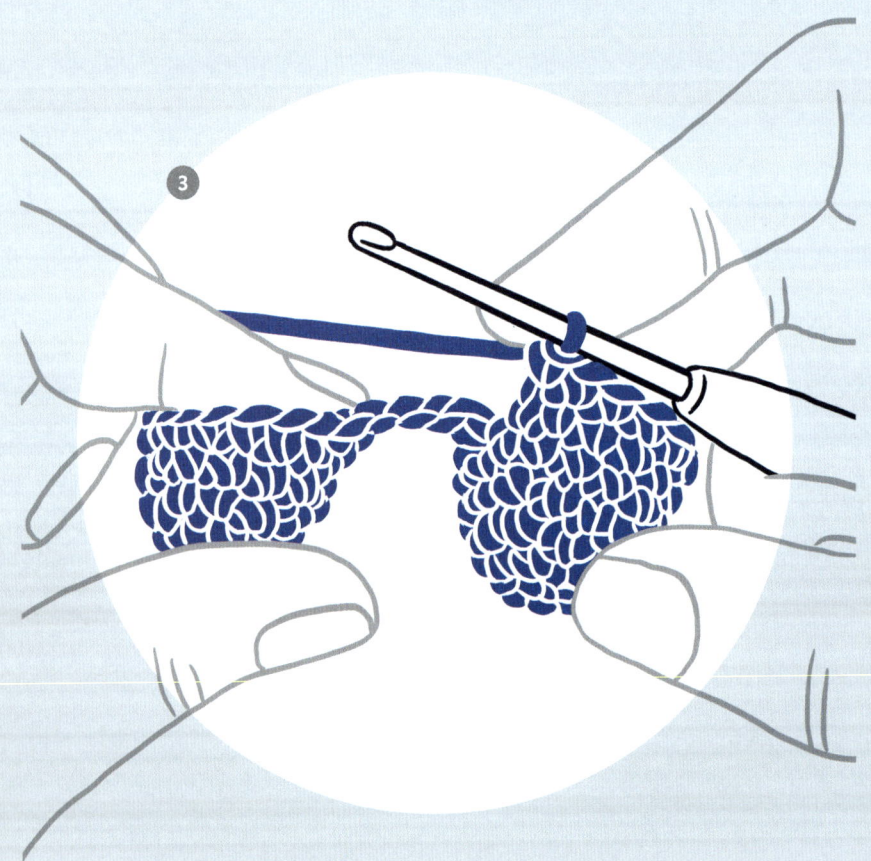

3 Work a single crochet stitch into the back loop only of each of the 3 chain stitches.

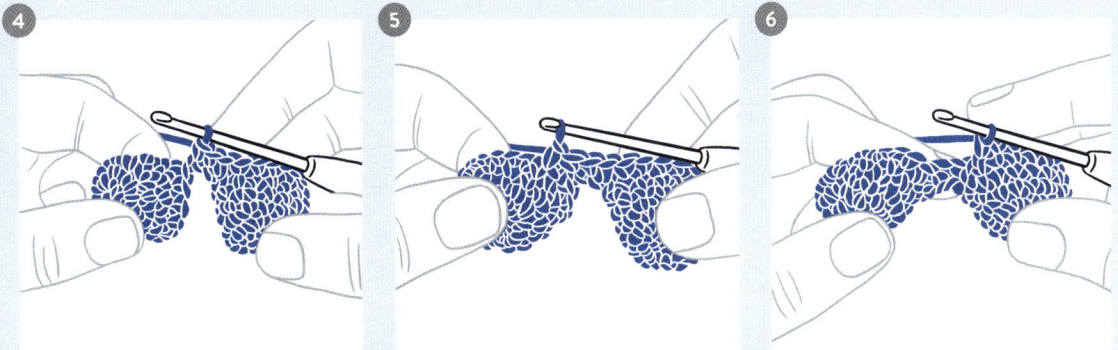

4 Insert the hook into the first stitch of the last round of the second piece. Work a single crochet stitch.

5 Work a single crochet stitch into each of the remaining stitches of the second piece until you reach the end of the round and the 3 chain stitches.

6 Work the next three single crochet stitches into the other side of the 3 chain stitches.

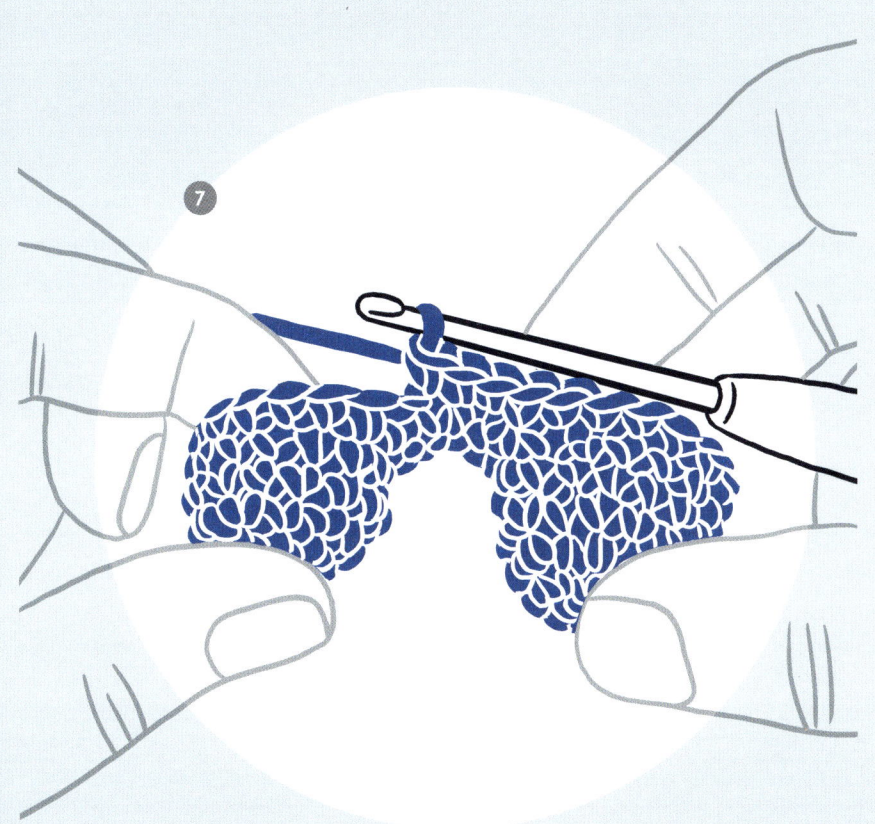

7 Continue to crochet in a spiral as instructed by the pattern.

Crochet stitches & other techniques

FINISHING TECHNIQUES

Adding stuffing to fill out a piece and embellishing the piece with extra details, such as facial features and accessories, is what really brings our amigurumi to life. It makes the biggest difference to how the finished amigurumi will look.

STUFFING

Stuffing is such an important part of the process as it greatly affects the final shape of the finished piece. Not enough stuffing can cause the final piece to be uneven in shape, while too much stuffing can stretch the stitches and create gaps in the crocheted fabric, so that the stuffing is visible. The finished piece should feel firm and smooth with no visible gaps between stitches.

To avoid bumps and an uneven finish, pull apart any clumps of stuffing and only add very small amounts at a time. For larger amigurumi pieces, focus on stuffing toward the sides of the piece before filling the centre. Use your hands to gently roll and manipulate the piece to distribute the stuffing evenly and feel for any soft spots that need more stuffing.

The pattern will usually instruct you when to begin stuffing and may even tell you how firmly to stuff each piece. Some pieces may not require any stuffing at all. If a pattern doesn't specify to what extent a piece should be stuffed, assume that the pieces are to be stuffed firmly.

Generally, you want to start stuffing the piece while it has a large enough opening. For long, thin pieces, such as arms and legs, it's important to start adding stuffing early to make sure the whole length is evenly stuffed. You can continue to add small amounts of stuffing as you work, but as the opening becomes smaller, it is useful to have something like a chopstick or even the blunt end of your crochet hook to help get the stuffing in there.

FASTENING OFF

Fastening off means cutting the working yarn and securing the end so that the piece doesn't unravel. This will look different depending on the project, so always check the pattern to see if you need to leave a long yarn tail for sewing pieces together. When it comes to sewing, a good rule of thumb is to leave a yarn tail approximately twice as long as the last round of the piece. Otherwise, always leave a yarn tail that's long enough to weave in comfortably – 6 inches (15cm) should suffice.

Fastening off a piece worked in rows

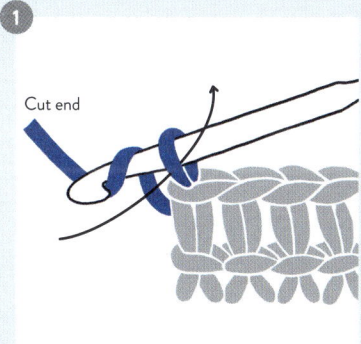

1 Work 1 chain. Leaving a yarn tail for sewing, if needed, cut the working yarn. Without removing the hook from the active loop, pull the hook away from the piece until the cut end of the yarn tail is pulled through the last stitch and there is no loop left on the hook.

2 Holding the chain, gently pull on the yarn tail to tighten the chain into a small knot. If you do not require a long yarn tail for sewing, weave in the end (see page 81).

Finishing techniques

Finishing off a flat/open piece worked in the round

As most amigurumi are worked in a continuous spiral without joining, you'll be left with a noticeable step or jog between the start and the end of the final round. To minimize this and give a smoother edge, use a finishing technique known as the invisible fasten off or invisible finish.

1 Work all the required stitches for the last round. Leaving a long yarn tail for sewing, if needed, cut the working yarn. Without removing the hook from the active loop, pull the hook away from the piece until the cut end of the yarn tail is pulled through the last stitch and there is no loop left on the hook.

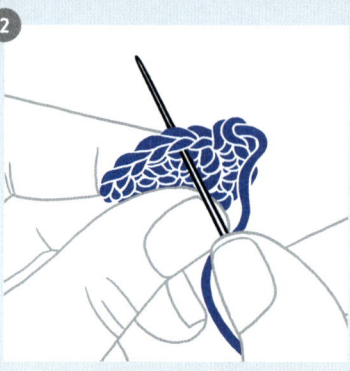

2 Thread the yarn tail onto a yarn needle. Skip the first stitch and insert the needle from front to back under both loops of the next stitch. Pull the yarn through.

3 Insert the needle from front to back through the back loop of the stitch the yarn tail is coming out from. Pull the yarn through to create a false stitch.

4 Tighten the false stitch by gently pulling on the yarn tail until it mimics the size of your other stitches. If you do not require a long yarn tail for sewing, weave in the end (see page 81).

Fastening off a closed piece

When you're making a closed piece, such as a sphere, you'll be left with a small hole after the final round. Most patterns simply tell you to fasten off, but don't specify how to close up that small hole to create a neat finish.

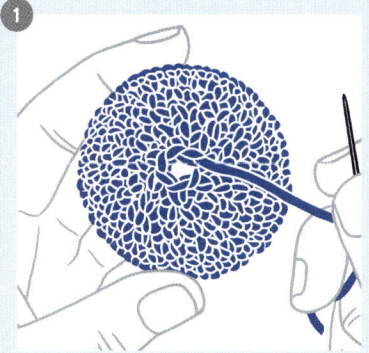

1 Cut the working yarn, leaving a yarn tail of about 6 inches (15cm). Pull the cut end of the yarn tail through the last stitch and thread it onto a yarn needle.

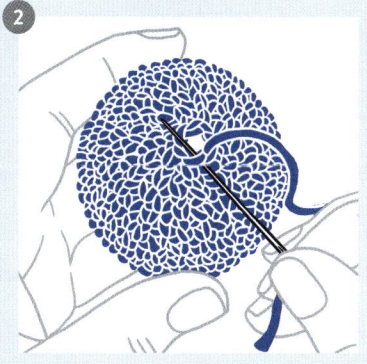

2 Insert the needle through the front loop only of the first stitch of the last round, from the outside to the inside.

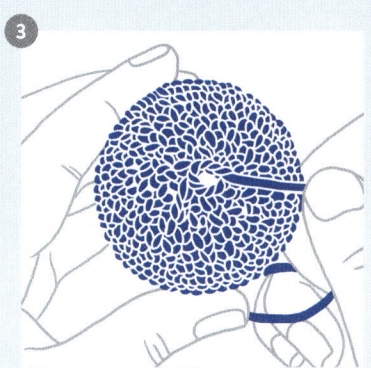

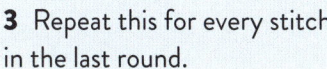

3 Repeat this for every stitch in the last round.

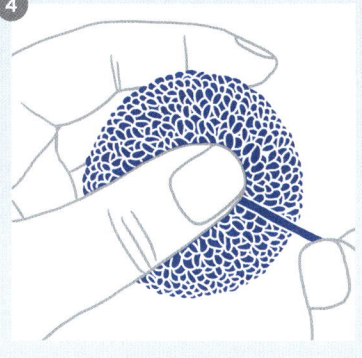

4 Place your thumb over the small hole and gently pull on the yarn tail to close the hole.

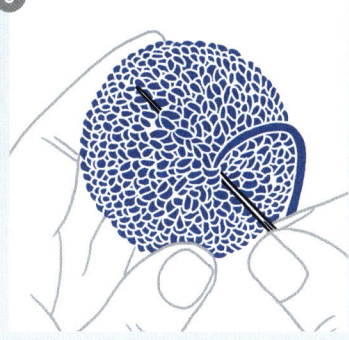

5 To finish, insert the needle through the centre of the hole that was just cinched closed and bring it out at a different place in the piece.

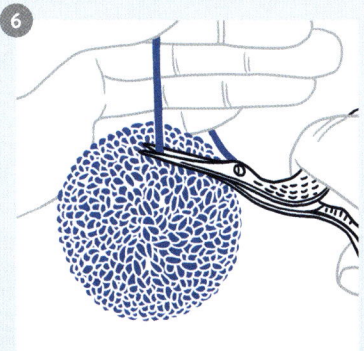

6 Pull the yarn tail taut and cut it close to the surface – the cut end will shrink back inside the piece.

Finishing techniques

SEWING TECHNIQUES

Many crocheters have a love-hate relationship when it comes to sewing pieces together. While no-sew patterns are on the rise, they don't allow for the same level of detail as patterns that incorporate some sewing. No-sew patterns aren't always as beginner-friendly either, as they often require more advanced crochet techniques or extra steps. I'll be the first to admit that sewing isn't my favourite part of the amigurumi process, however it's an important skill to learn and gets easier with practice. The plus side is that you won't be so limited in your pattern choices.

Sewing an open piece to another open piece
This method of sewing two open pieces together creates a tidy, invisible seam.

1 Hold or pin the two open ends together in the correct position. Thread the yarn tail onto a yarn needle.

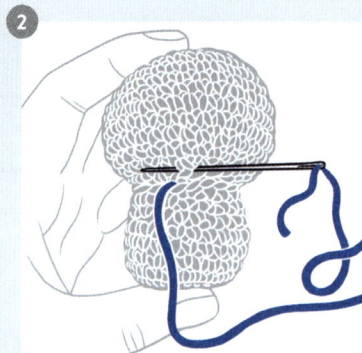

2 Insert the needle behind the vertical bar of the stitch directly opposite the yarn tail on the opposing piece. Draw the yarn through.

3 Insert the needle back into the same stitch that the yarn tail is coming out from on the original piece and behind the vertical bar of the next stitch. Draw the yarn through.

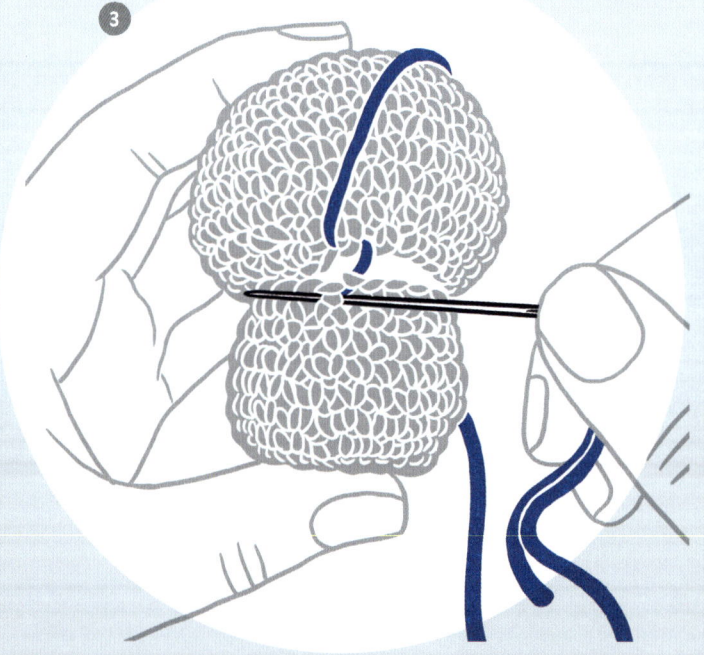

> **TIP**
> It's easier to see what you're doing if you don't draw the yarn tight after every stitch.

Stitches, techniques & finishing

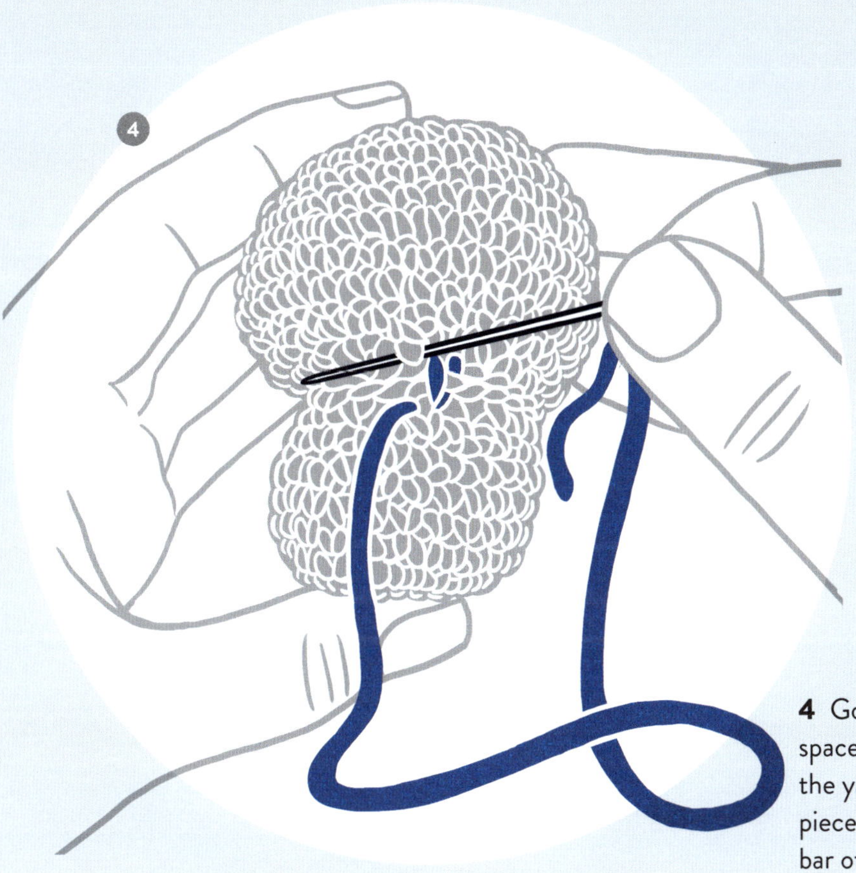

4 Go back into the same space where you last brought the yarn up on the opposing piece and behind the vertical bar of the next stitch. Draw the yarn through.

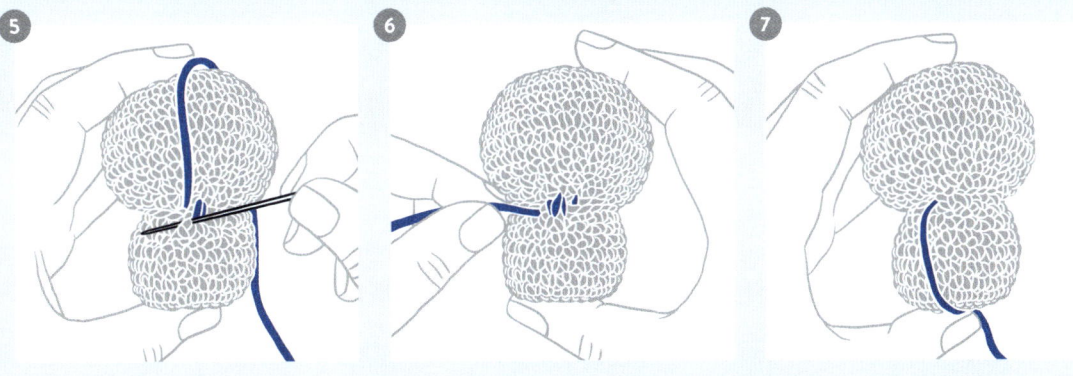

5 Repeat step 3.

6 Grab the yarn tail and pull it as tight as you can until the stitches disappear.

7 Repeat steps 4–6 until you reach the end.

Finishing techniques

Sewing an open piece to a closed piece

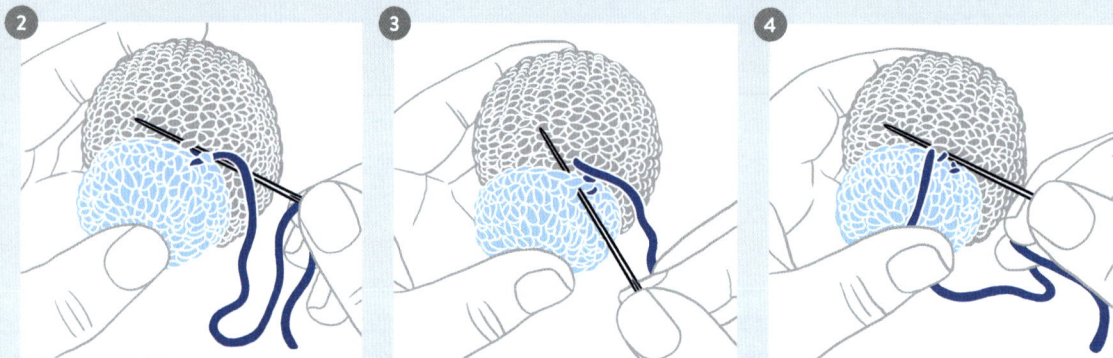

1 Pin the open piece to the closed piece in the correct position. Thread the yarn tail onto a yarn needle.

2 Insert the needle through a stitch on the closed piece just above the yarn tail. Draw the yarn tight.

3 Insert the needle through the next stitch of the open piece, going under both loops from front to back.

4 Insert the needle back into the same space that you brought the yarn up in step 2 and through the next stitch. Draw the yarn tight.

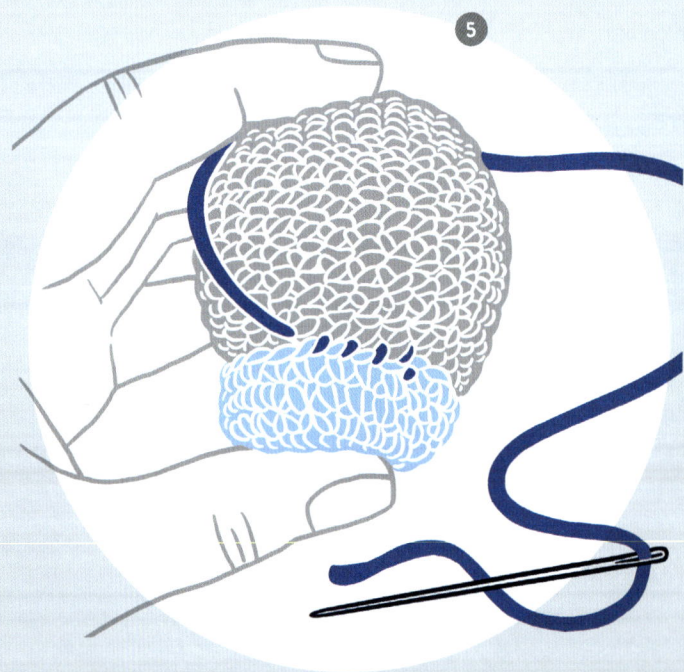

5 Continue stitching around the open piece, drawing the yarn tight after each stitch.

Sewing a flat piece to a closed piece

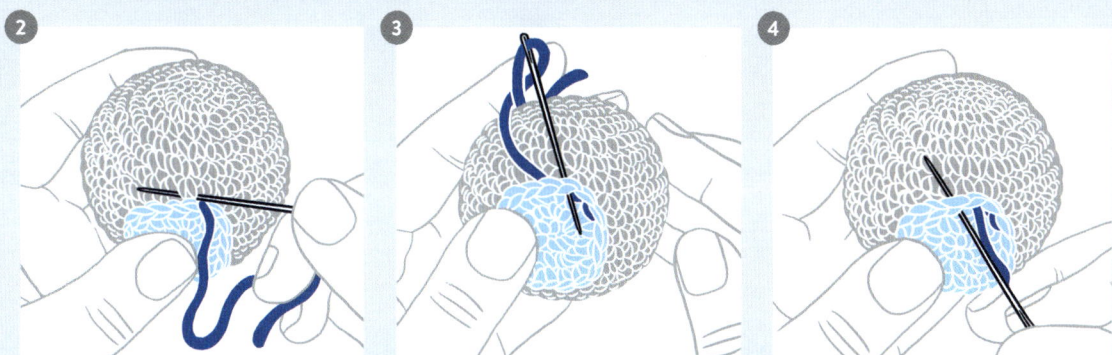

1 Pin the flat piece to the closed piece in the correct position. Thread the yarn tail onto a yarn needle.

2 Insert the needle through a stitch on the closed piece directly below the yarn tail.

3 Insert the needle under both loops of the flat piece from the bottom up, directly above where it came out of the closed piece.

4 Insert the needle under both loops of the next stitch of the flat piece from the top down.

5 Insert the needle through a stitch of the closed piece, directly below where it came out of the flat piece.

6 Repeat steps 3–5 until you have sewn around the entire flat piece.

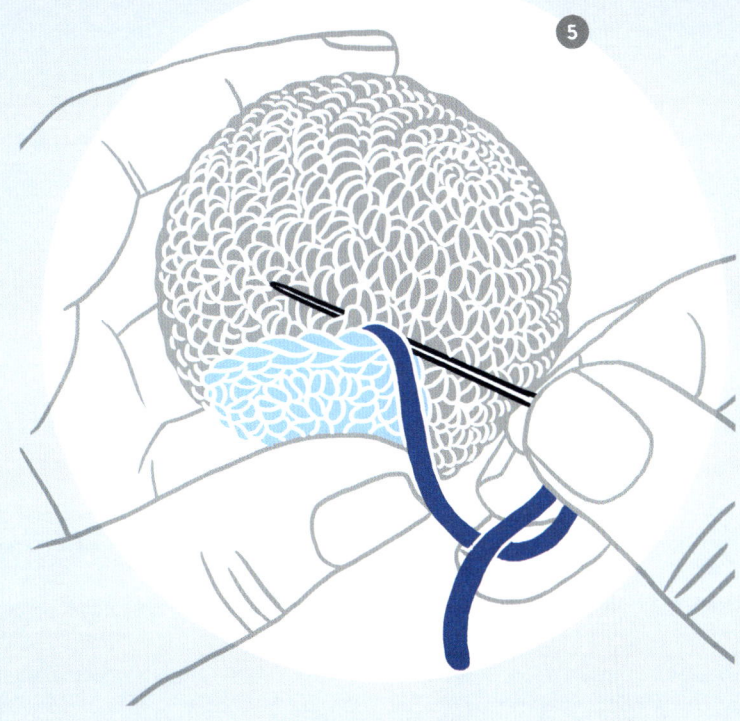

Finishing techniques 79

Sewing a finished edge piece to a closed piece

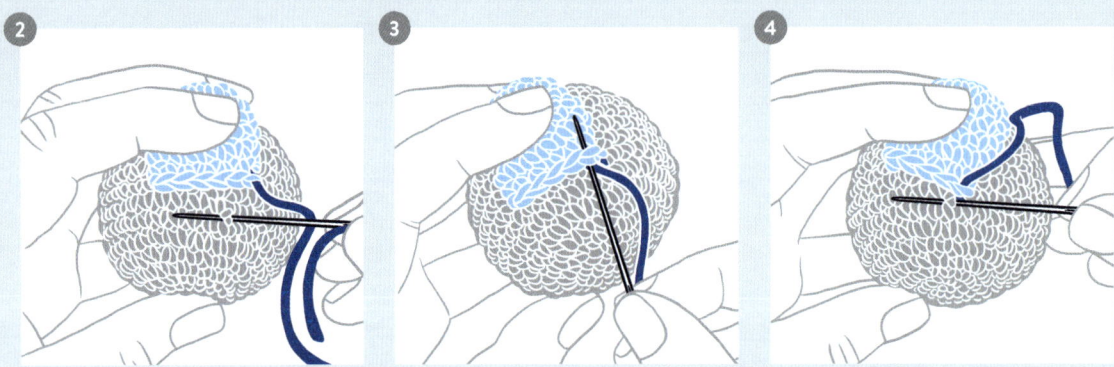

1 Pin the finished edge piece to the closed piece in the correct position. Thread the yarn tail onto a yarn needle.

2 Insert the needle through a stitch just below the first stitch of the finished edge piece.

3 Insert the needle under both loops of the finished edge piece from back to front directly above where it came out of the closed piece.

4 Insert the needle back into the same space that you brought the yarn up in step 2 and out through the next stitch. Draw the stitch tight.

5 Repeat steps 3–4 across the top of the finished edge piece.

6 When you get to the last stitch, insert the needle back into the same space that the yarn is coming out of and bring it out at a different place in the piece.

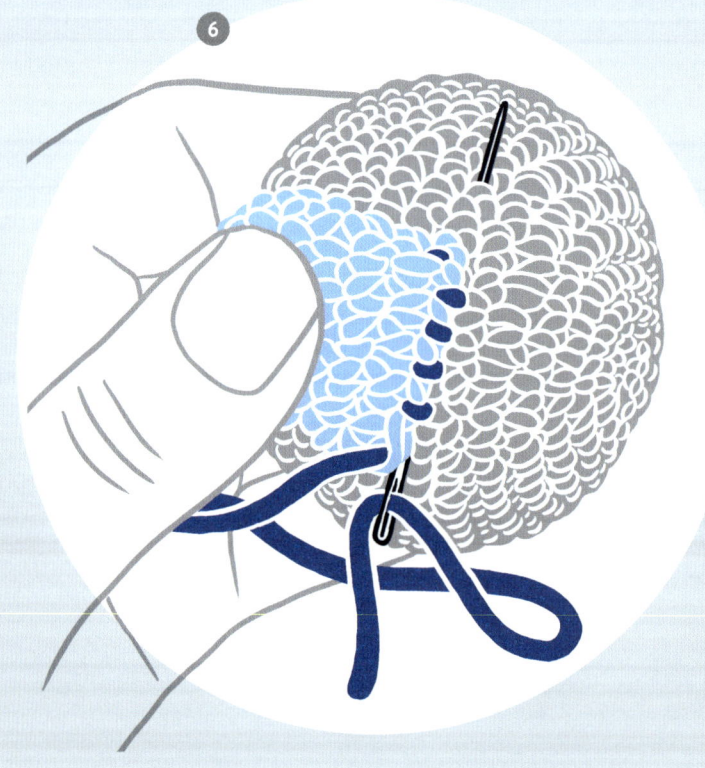

WEAVING IN YARN ENDS

After sewing all the pieces of your amigurumi in place, you'll need to weave in any yarn ends. Weaving in yarn ends is the term used for securing any loose cut ends of yarn and is an essential part of any crochet project. How many ends you have to weave in and how you weave in your ends is dependent on the finished piece.

TIP
Don't pull the yarn too tight to avoid pulling the piece out of shape. When you're finished, simply snip the remaining yarn tail as close as possible to the finished piece, being careful not to cut the fabric itself.

Weaving in yarn ends on flat pieces
For flat pieces, you need to weave the yarn tail through the crochet stitches on the wrong side of your work.

1 Thread the yarn tail onto a yarn needle. Weave the yarn needle under your last row of stitches for about 2 inches (5cm).

2 Skip a stitch, then bring the yarn needle back through the same stitches in that row.

3 For extra security, drop down a row and repeat the process.

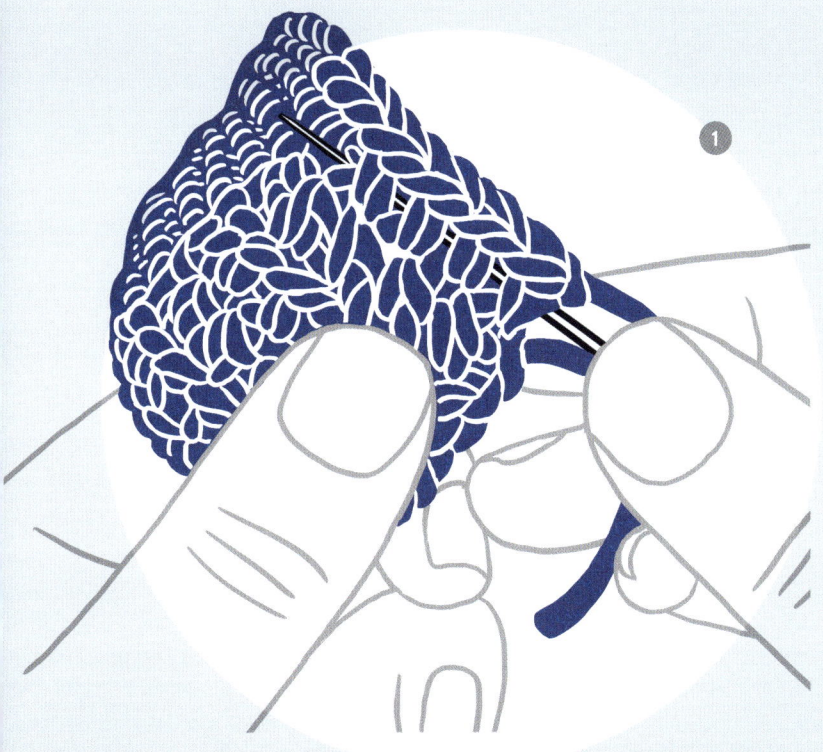

Weaving in yarn ends in amigurumi

When weaving in a single yarn tail:

1 Thread the yarn tail onto a yarn needle. Insert the needle into the same space that the yarn is coming out of and bring it out somewhere else on the finished piece.

2 Repeat step 1 a few times, coming out at a different place each time.

3 Pull the yarn tail taut and snip it close to the surface. The cut end will shrink back inside the finished piece.

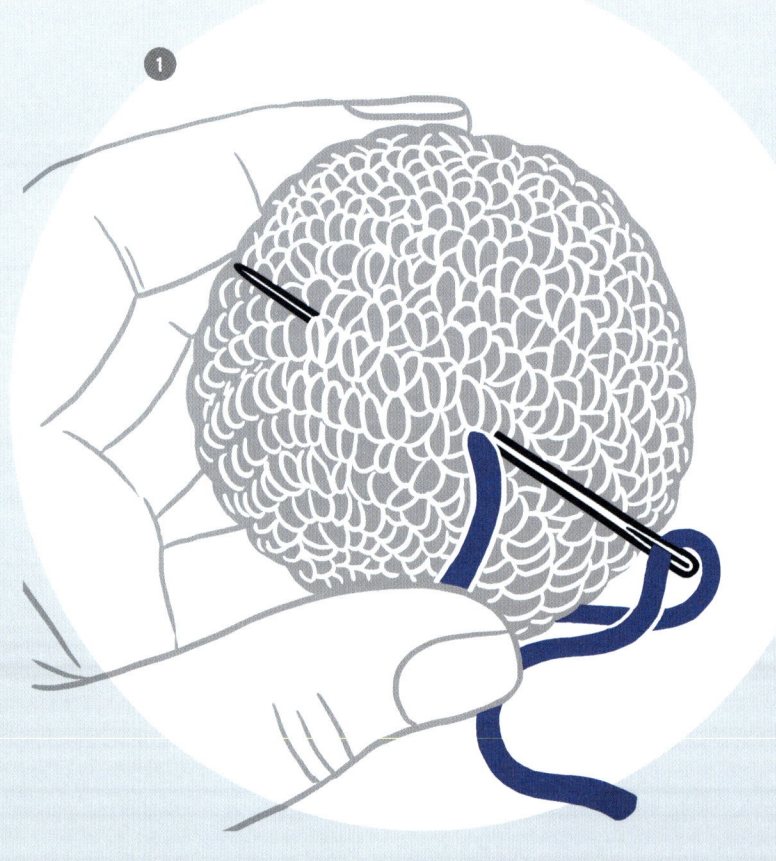

When weaving in multiple yarn tails:

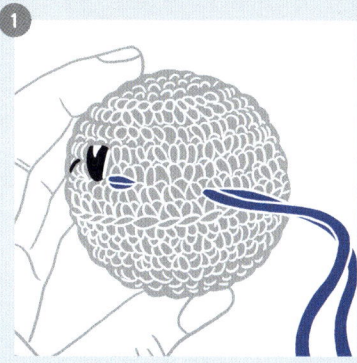

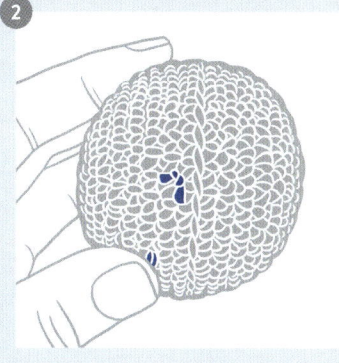

NOTE
When sewing body parts in pairs, such as arms, legs and ears, always secure the yarn tails of the two pieces together before weaving in.

1 Bring two yarn tails out through the same space on the finished piece.

2 Tie the tails together in a double knot and trim away any excess.

3 Using the end of a yarn needle or sharp pair of tweezers, push the knot down into the finished piece.

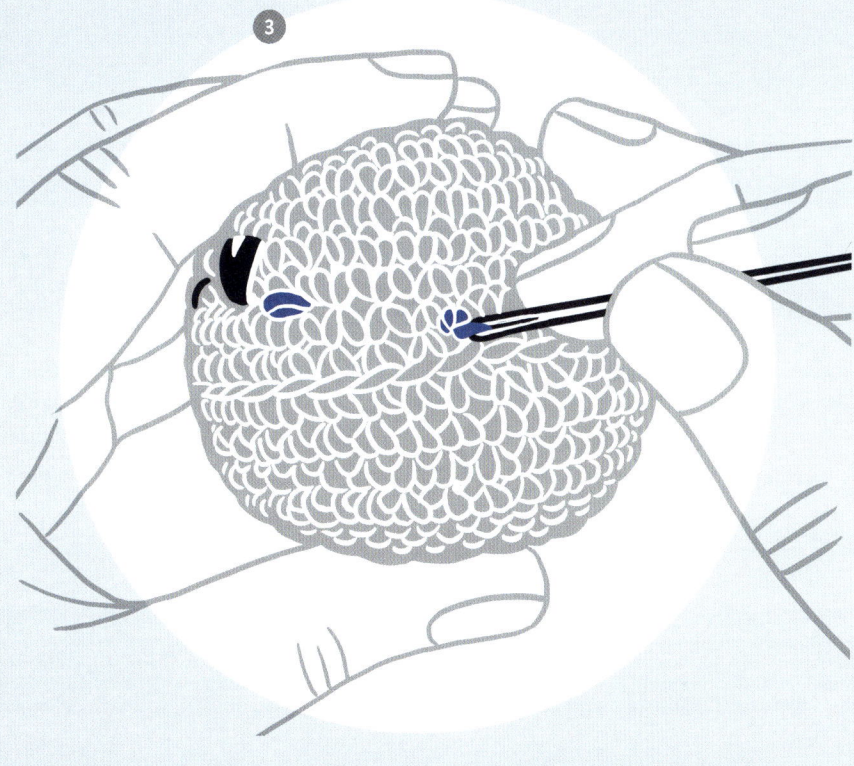

Finishing techniques

ADDING FACIAL DETAILS

Facial details can make or break a project. It's the final step in bringing your creations to life and gives them so much personality. Amigurumi pieces are often quite small, so there's not a lot of room for detail. I like to take the less-is-more approach and I encourage you to do the same as simple facial features make the characters look cute without overwhelming the piece.

Adding safety eyes

Safety eyes are made up of two components: the eye itself that sits on the outside of the piece and the washer that snaps onto the back inside the piece to lock the eye in place.

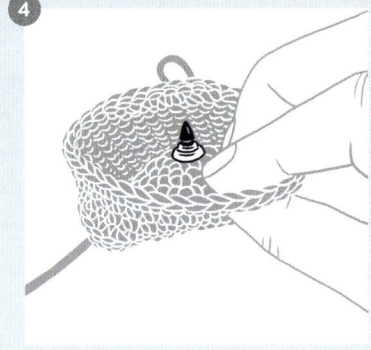

TIPS
- Always use pins to mark out the placement of the safety eyes first, then make any adjustments as needed.
- If your crochet stitches are very tight, use a crochet hook to make a bigger space to slip the safety eye into.
- Double check the positioning of the safety eyes and make sure that they're in the correct place before attaching the washers on the back.
- Don't be afraid to use bigger or smaller safety eyes and adjust their positioning according to your own personal preference.

1 Mark the positions of each eye with pins. Place the first eye in the correct position on the outside of the piece according to the pattern instructions.

2 Insert the post of the eye part between two stitches.

3 Place the second eye in the correct position by counting over the required number of stitches stated in the pattern. For example, if the pattern states to place the eyes 5 stitches apart, count over 5 stitches and place the eye in the 6th stitch.

4 Place the washer over the post of the first eye, on the inside of the piece with the flat side facing the crocheted fabric. Push down on both sides of the washer until it snaps into place. Make sure that the eye is secure but doesn't distort the piece.

5 Repeat for the second eye.

Stitches, techniques & finishing

Adding simple embroidered eyes
Despite the name, safety eyes aren't recommended for children under the age of 3 as they do present a choking hazard. Embroidered eyes are a suitable safe alternative. Simple embroidered eyes are an ideal substitute for plain black safety eyes and give a similar look.

1 Use pins to mark out the placement of the embroidered eyes. Place the first pin in the same spot that the safety eye would go and the second pin into a stitch directly above or below the first pin. Decide which position you prefer. Once you're happy with the placement, cut a 12-inch (30-cm) length of black embroidery floss/thread and thread it onto a yarn needle.

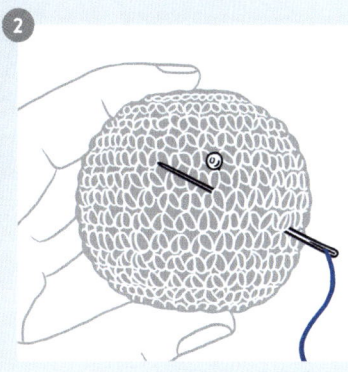

2 For the first eye, insert the needle through a stitch at the side of the piece and then bring it up through the stitch marked by the bottom pin. Leave a 4-inch (10-cm) tail for weaving in later.

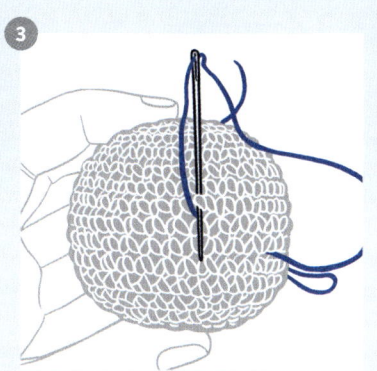

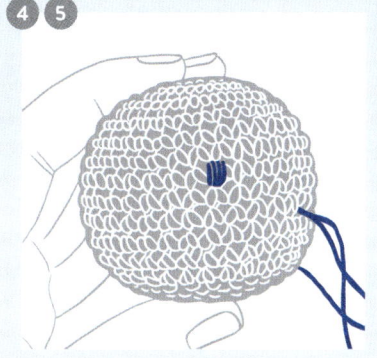

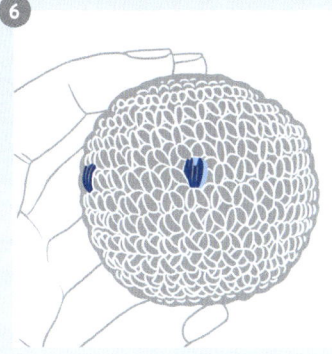

3 Insert the needle down through the stitch marked by the top pin, then bring it out again where the bottom pin was.

4 Repeat step 3, placing the stitches so that they lie next to each other and create a dense black dot with no gaps. Continue until you're happy with the fullness of the eye.

5 For the last stitch, bring the yarn needle out through the same space as your starting tail. Weave in the yarn ends.

6 Repeat steps 2–5 for the second eye. Make exactly the same number of stitches for both eyes so that they're identical in size. If you're feeling adventurous, add a single stitch of white to the outer edge of the eye and a short stitch to the centre.

Finishing techniques

Adding cheeks

Cheeks are one of the simplest details that you can add to up the cuteness factor of your creations. You can crochet two separate circles and sew these onto your character or embroider a series of straight stitches onto the amigurumi using embroidery floss/thread.

1 To add simple embroidered cheeks, start by cutting a 12-inch (30-cm) length of pink yarn or embroidery floss and threading it onto a yarn needle.

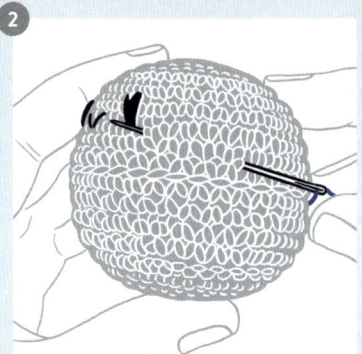

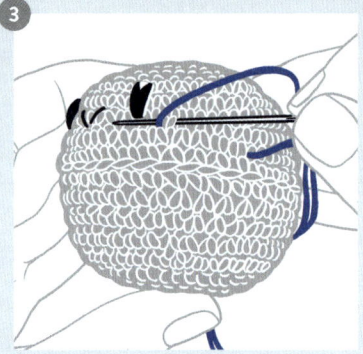

2 Insert the needle through a stitch at the side of the piece and then bring it up through a stitch beneath and slightly to the side of the eye. Leave a 4-inch (10-cm) tail for weaving in later.

3 Insert the needle one stitch across, away from the eye, and then bring it back up again through the same hole that the yarn is coming out of.

> **TIP**
> If the yarn needle doesn't reach all the way across, bring it out part way and then take it the rest of the way across or sew each cheek individually.

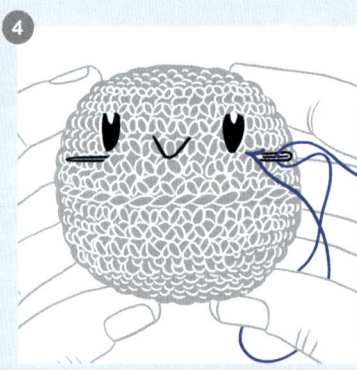

4 Insert the needle one stitch across again, through the same stitch as before, and then bring it back up again under and slightly to the side of the other eye.

5 Repeat step 3.

6 Insert the needle one stitch across again, through the same space as before, and then bring it back up again through the same stitch as your starting tail. Weave in the yarn ends.

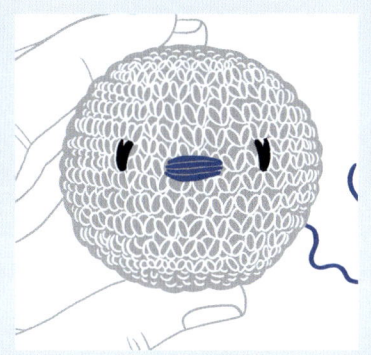

Adding noses
A simple nose can be made by sewing straight stitches, in the same way as when adding cheeks and eyes, but over a longer span of stitches. Always insert and then bring the needle up through the same hole. Keep stitching until you have achieved your desired effect and thickness.

Adding mouths
The simplest mouth is a small embroidered V shape positioned between the eyes.

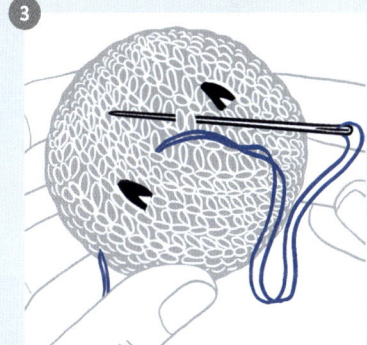

1 Use pins to mark out the placement of the mouth. Mark the three points of the V. Once you're happy with the placement, cut a 12-inch (30-cm) length of black embroidery floss/thread, separate out two strands and thread both strands onto an embroidery needle.

2 Insert the needle through a stitch to the side of the right eye and then bring it up through the stitch marked by the first pin. Leave a 4-inch (10-cm) tail for weaving in later.

3 Take the needle across and down, then insert it through the stitch marked by the second pin. Bring it out again at the third pin. You'll now have a straight line between the eyes.

TIP
Run the tip of the yarn needle under the stitches to help them lay flat and don't pull the embroidered stitches too tight.

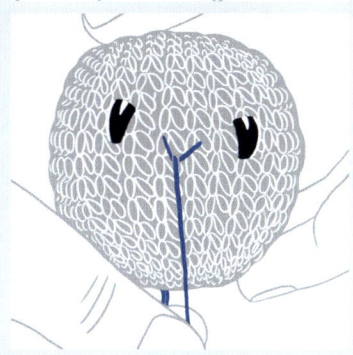

4 Insert the needle under that straight stitch and pull gently downwards to create a V shape.

5 Insert the needle back down through the same stitch where the embroidery floss is coming out of and out through the same space as the starting tail. Weave in the yarn ends.

Finishing techniques

ADDING EMBROIDERED KNOTS

Knots are another way of adding detail and can be used for eyes, noses or simply adding texture.

Adding French knots
A French knot is an embroidery technique that makes a small knot directly on the surface of a piece. These embroidered knots can be used as an alternative for eyes, cheeks or any other details that you can think of.

1 Cut a 12-inch (30-cm) length of black embroidery floss/thread and thread it onto a yarn needle.

2 Insert the needle through a stitch at the side and then bring it up through the stitch where you want to place the knot.

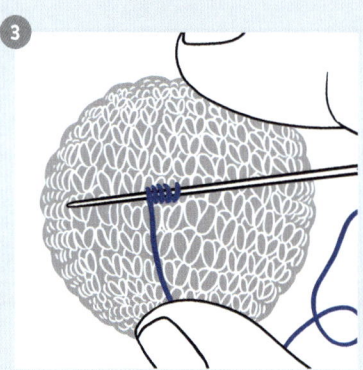

3 Lay the needle behind the thread and wrap the thread around the needle three times.

4 Take the needle partway down through your piece, close to where the thread is coming out, then slowly pull the needle and working thread through the wraps to complete the French knot.

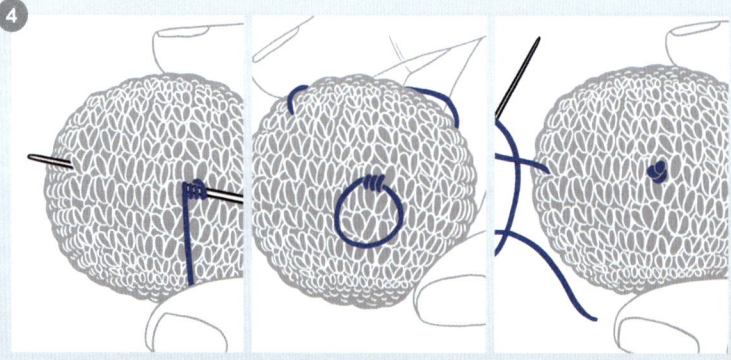

> **TIP**
> You can change the size of the French knots by wrapping the thread around the needle more times or by using something thicker like yarn.

> **EMBROIDERY TIPS**
>
> When it comes to using embroidery for adding detail, keep the following things in mind:
>
> • Use a sharp needle.
>
> • Use finer yarn or embroidery floss/thread to build up definition through layered stitches.
>
> • Don't pull your embroidered stitches too tight.

Adding wrap knots

A wrap knot is similar to a French knot but is made without the needle. Each knot is created from a length of yarn before being attached to the piece.

In this example, we'll make a 6-wrap knot. The more wraps you make, the bigger the knot will be.

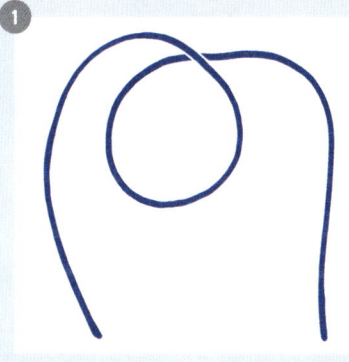

1 Cut a 12-inch (30-cm) length of yarn and make a loop in the middle.

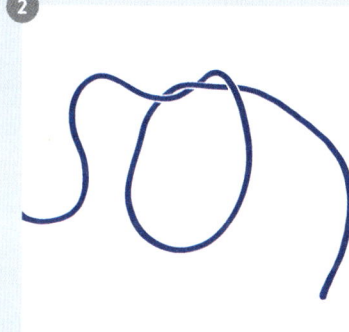

2 Pass one end of the yarn through the loop as if tying a knot.

3 Repeat step 2 a further five times.

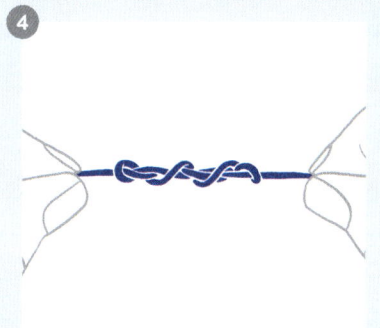

4 Slowly pull both ends of the yarn – the loops will start to align and shrink down into a knot – but avoid pulling the knot too tight.

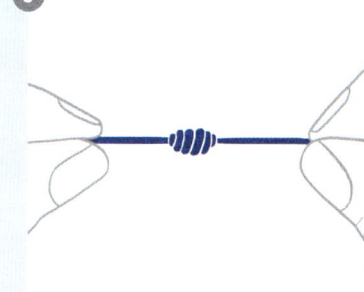

5 Use the yarn ends to secure the knot to your amigurumi.

PATTERNS

Now that we've covered the basics, it's time to put your new skills into action. In this section, you'll find a collection of fun amigurumi patterns, progressing in order of difficulty, to help you practice and grow your confidence stitch by stitch.

POTATO

Who doesn't love potatoes? A crochet potato is a great place to start your amigurumi journey as their naturally irregular shape is perfect for hiding any mistakes or uneven tension. It's an easy and fun way to practise some basic stitches and an opportunity to build confidence in your crochet skills.

FINISHED SIZE

Approximately 3 inches (8cm) tall by 2 inches (5cm) wide.

Size may vary depending on your gauge/tension and the yarn used.

MATERIALS

- Paintbox Yarns Cotton Aran or any other worsted/aran-weight yarn in beige (Vanilla Cream) and a small amount of pink (Bubblegum Pink)
- 3.5mm (US E/4) crochet hook
- Pair of 8mm black safety eyes
- Polyester fibre filling or any other fire-safe toy stuffing
- Black embroidery floss/thread
- Stitch marker
- Scissors
- Yarn needle
- Embroidery needle

PATTERN NOTES

• This pattern is worked in the round in a continuous spiral.

• Mark the first stitch of each round with a movable stitch marker.

GAUGE/TENSION

Gauge is not important in this pattern. Use a hook size to match your chosen yarn and make sure that your stitches are tight enough to prevent stuffing showing through. Adjust hook size if necessary.

ABBREVIATIONS

ch – chain
inc – increase
invdec – invisible decrease
mr – magic ring
R – round or row
sc – single crochet
st(s) – stitch(es)

[...] – repeat the instructions inside the square brackets

(...) – indicates the stitch count at the end of the round or row

POTATO
Using beige yarn, make a magic ring.

R1: 6 sc in mr (6)
R2: [Inc] x6 (12)
R3: [Sc, inc] x6 (18)
R4: Sc, inc, [2 sc, inc] x5, sc (24)
R5: [Sc] x24 (24)
R6: [3 sc, inc] x6 (30)
R7–10: [Sc] x30 (30)
4 rounds
R11: 2 sc, inc, [4 sc, inc] x5, 2 sc (36)
R12–17: [Sc] x36 (36)
6 rounds
R18: 2 sc, invdec, [4 sc, invdec] x5, 2 sc (30)
R19: [3 sc, invdec] x6 (24)

Position the safety eyes between R8 and R9, 5 sts apart. Fix in place.

Start stuffing and continue to stuff as you work.

R20: Sc, invdec, [2 sc, invdec] x5, sc (18)
R21: [Sc, invdec] x6 (12)
R22: [Invdec] x6 (6)

Cut the working yarn, leaving a long tail. Pull the yarn tail through the last stitch.

Weave the yarn tail through the front loops only of the final round and gently pull to close the opening.

Hide any yarn ends inside the potato.

FINISHING DETAILS
Using two strands of black embroidery floss/thread, sew a V shape over R9 positioned between the eyes for the mouth.

Using pink yarn, sew a cheek just under and to the side of each eye by making two horizontal stitches over a single stitch.

SOUR LEMON

This sour lemon is cute and fun. Since lemons are naturally a little bumpy and imperfect, this is a forgiving project to continue practising working in the round and basic shaping.
It's also an opportunity to try some simple embellishment with the optional addition of crochet cheeks.

FINISHED SIZE

Approximately 3¼ inches (8.5cm) long by 2 inches (5cm) wide.

Size may vary depending on your gauge/tension and the yarn used.

MATERIALS

- Paintbox Yarns Cotton Aran or any other worsted/aran-weight yarn in light yellow (Daffodil Yellow) and a small amount of pink (Bubblegum Pink)
- 3.5mm (US E/4) crochet hook
- Pair of 8mm black safety eyes
- Polyester fibre filling or any other fire-safe toy stuffing
- Black embroidery floss/thread
- Stitch marker
- Scissors
- Yarn needle
- Embroidery needle

PATTERN NOTES

- This pattern is worked in the round in a continuous spiral.
- Mark the first stitch of each round with a movable stitch marker.
- The crocheted cheeks are optional. Feel free to embroider the cheeks instead (as for the potato on page 95).

ABBREVIATIONS

ch – chain
inc – increase
invdec – invisible decrease
mr – magic ring
R – round or row
sc – single crochet
st(s) – stitch(es)

[...] – repeat the instructions inside the square brackets

(...) – indicates the stitch count at the end of the round or row

GAUGE/TENSION

Gauge is not important in this pattern. Use a hook size to match your chosen yarn and make sure that your stitches are tight enough to prevent stuffing showing through. Adjust hook size if necessary.

SOUR LEMON

Using light yellow yarn, make a magic ring.

R1: 6 sc in mr (6)
R2: [Sc] x6 (6)
R3: [Inc] x6 (12)
R4: [Sc, inc] x6 (18)
R5: Sc, inc, [2 sc, inc] x5, sc (24)
R6: [3 sc, inc] x6 (30)
R7: 2 sc, inc, [4 sc, inc] x5, 2 sc (36)
R8–17: [Sc] x36 (36)
10 rounds
R18: 2 sc, invdec, [4 sc, invdec] x5, 2 sc (30)
R19: [3 sc, invdec] x6 (24)

Position the first safety eye between R8 and R9 and the second eye between R16 and R17. Make sure they are in line with each other. Fix in place.

Start stuffing and continue to stuff as you work.

R20: Sc, invdec, [2 sc, invdec] x5, sc (18)
R21: [Sc, invdec] x6 (12)
R22: [Invdec] x6 (6)
R23: [Sc] x6 (6)

Cut the working yarn, leaving a long tail. Pull the yarn tail through the last stitch.

Weave the yarn tail through the front loops only of the final round and gently pull to close the opening.

Hide any yarn ends inside the sour lemon.

CHEEKS
(MAKE 2 – OPTIONAL)
Using pink yarn, make a magic ring.

R1: 6 sc in mr (6)

Fasten off invisibly, leaving a long yarn tail for sewing.

FINISHING DETAILS

Using the yarn tail, sew the cheeks in place just below and to the side of each eye.

Using two strands of black embroidery floss/thread, sew a straight line over about 4 rounds positioned between the eyes for the mouth.

PENCIL

This amigurumi pencil is a one-piece pattern that's perfect for practising stitch consistency, working in the back loop only and simple colour changes. You could also change up the colours to turn it from a pencil into a crayon. It makes a super-cute back-to-school or teacher gift.

FINISHED SIZE

Approximately 3¾ inches (9.5cm) long by 1½ inches (4cm) wide.

Size may vary depending on your gauge/tension and the yarn used.

MATERIALS

- Paintbox Yarns Cotton Aran or any other worsted/aran-weight yarn in light pink (Blush Pink), light grey (Stormy Grey), light yellow (Daffodil Yellow), beige (Vanilla Cream) and black (Pure Black)
- 3.5mm (US E/4) crochet hook
- Pair of 8mm black safety eyes
- Polyester fibre filling or any other fire-safe toy stuffing
- Card (you can use a cereal box, tissue box, etc.)
- Black embroidery floss/thread
- Stitch marker
- Scissors
- Yarn needle
- Embroidery needle

PATTERN NOTES

• This pattern is worked in the round in a continuous spiral.

• Mark the first stitch of each round with a movable stitch marker.

• All colour changes take place in the last yarn over of the previous colour.

• Round 5 is worked in the back loop only.

ABBREVIATIONS

BLO – back loop only
ch – chain
inc – increase
invdec – invisible decrease
mr – magic ring
R – round or row
sc – single crochet
st(s) – stitch(es)

[...] – repeat the instructions inside the square brackets

(...) – indicates the stitch count at the end of the round or row

GAUGE/TENSION

Gauge is not important in this pattern. Use a hook size to match your chosen yarn and make sure that your stitches are tight enough to prevent stuffing showing through. Adjust hook size if necessary.

PENCIL
Using light pink yarn, make a magic ring.

R1: 6 sc in mr (6)
R2: [Inc] x6 (12)
R3: [Sc, inc] x6 (18)
R4: Sc, inc, [2 sc, inc] x5, sc (24)
R5: Work the entire round in BLO – [sc] x24 (24)
R6–7: [Sc] x24 (24) *2 rounds*

Change to light grey yarn in the last stitch of R7.

Measure the diameter of the pencil top and cut a circle out of card the same dimensions. Place it inside the pencil.

R8: [Sc] x24 (24)

Change to light yellow yarn in the last stitch of R8.

R9–18: [Sc] x24 (24) *10 rounds*

Change to beige yarn in the last stitch of R18.

Position the safety eyes between R14 and R15, 5 sts apart. Fix in place.

Start stuffing and continue to stuff as you work.

R19: [Sc] x24 (24)
R20: Sc, invdec, [2 sc, invdec] x5, sc (18)
R21: [Sc] x18 (18)
R22: [Sc, invdec] x6 (12)

Change to black yarn in the last stitch of R22.

R23–24: [Sc] x12 (12) *2 rounds*
R25: [Invdec] x6 (6)

Cut the working yarn, leaving a long tail. Pull the yarn tail through the last stitch.

Weave the yarn tail through the front loops only of the final round and gently pull to close the opening.

Hide any yarn ends inside the pencil.

FINISHING DETAILS
Using two strands of black embroidery floss/thread, sew a V shape over R15 positioned between the eyes for the mouth.

PLANET

This adorable planet is a simple crocheted sphere. It's worked in the round with one round worked in the back loop only, leaving the front loop which is then crocheted into later to create the planet's rings. This little planet would make a sweet addition to a space-themed baby mobile for a nursery.

FINISHED SIZE

Approximately 2½ inches (6.5cm) tall by 3½ inches (9cm) wide.

Size may vary depending on your gauge/tension and the yarn used.

MATERIALS

- Paintbox Yarns Cotton Aran or any other worsted/aran-weight yarn in light blue (Duck Egg Blue), dark blue (Dolphin Blue) and a small amount of pink (Bubblegum Pink)
- 3.5mm (US E/4) crochet hook
- Pair of 8mm black safety eyes
- Polyester fibre filling or any other fire-safe toy stuffing
- Black embroidery floss/thread
- Stitch marker
- Scissors
- Yarn needle
- Embroidery needle

PATTERN NOTES

• This pattern is worked in the round in a continuous spiral.

• Mark the first stitch of each round with a movable stitch marker.

• Round 11 of the planet is worked in the back loop only.

• Round 1 of the rings is worked into the leftover front loops from Round 11.

GAUGE/TENSION

Gauge is not important in this pattern. Use a hook size to match your chosen yarn and make sure that your stitches are tight enough to prevent stuffing showing through. Adjust hook size if necessary.

ABBREVIATIONS

BLO – back loop only
ch – chain
inc – increase
invdec – invisible decrease
mr – magic ring
R – round or row
sc – single crochet
st(s) – stitch(es)
sl st – slip stitch
[…] – repeat the instructions inside the square brackets
(…) – indicates the stitch count at the end of the round or row

PLANET

Using light blue yarn, make a magic ring.

R1: 6 sc in mr (6)
R2: [Inc] x6 (12)
R3: [Sc, inc] x6 (18)
R4: Sc, inc, [2 sc, inc] x5, sc (24)
R5: [3 sc, inc] x6 (30)
R6: 2 sc, inc, [4 sc, inc] x5, 2 sc (36)
R7–10: [Sc] x36 (36)
4 rounds
R11: Work the entire round in BLO – [sc] x36 (36)
R12–14: [Sc] x36 (36)
3 rounds

Position the safety eyes between R7 and R8, 5 sts apart. Fix in place.

R15: 2 sc, invdec, [4 sc, invdec] x5, 2 sc (30)
R16: [3 sc, invdec] x6 (24)

Start stuffing and continue to stuff as you work.

R17: Sc, invdec, [2 sc, invdec] x5, sc (18)
R18: [Sc, invdec] x6 (12)
R19: [Invdec] x6 (6)

Cut the working yarn, leaving a long tail. Pull the yarn tail through the last stitch.

Weave the yarn tail through the front loops only of the final round and gently pull to close the opening.

Hide any yarn ends inside the planet.

RINGS

Work R1 of the rings into the leftover front loops from R11 of the planet.

Holding the planet upside down, join dark blue yarn to the first leftover front loop from R11.

R1: Ch 1, sc in same space, 2 sc, inc, [3 sc, inc] x8 (45)
R2: 2 sc, inc, [4 sc, inc] x 8, 2 sc (54)
R3: [5 sc, inc] x9 (63)
Sc in next st, sl st in next st.

Fasten off invisibly.

Weave in any yarn ends.

FINISHING DETAILS

Using two strands of black embroidery floss/thread, sew a V shape over R8 positioned between the eyes for the mouth.

Using pink yarn, sew a cheek just under and to the side of each eye by making two horizontal stitches over a single stitch.

MALLARD DUCK

The bands of colour make this little bird instantly recognizable as a mallard duck. The simple body shape allows you to keep practising stitch consistency and achieving an even tension. It's also a chance to try your hand at half double crochet stitches, which are worked around a foundation chain to create the wings. This is a great gift for the nature lovers in your life.

FINISHED SIZE

Approximately 2¾ inches (7cm) tall by 2¼ inches (6cm) wide, not including the wings.

Size may vary depending on your gauge/tension and the yarn used.

MATERIALS

- Paintbox Yarns Cotton Aran or any other worsted/aran-weight yarn in dark green (Racing Green), white (Paper White), dark brown (Coffee Bean) and yellow (Mustard Yellow)
- 3.5mm (US E/4) crochet hook
- Pair of 8mm black safety eyes
- Polyester fibre filling or any other fire-safe toy stuffing
- Stitch marker
- Scissors
- Yarn needle

PATTERN NOTES

• This pattern is worked in the round in a continuous spiral.

• Mark the first stitch of each round with a movable stitch marker.

• All colour changes take place in the last yarn over of the previous colour.

• The wings are worked around a foundation chain (see page 43).

ABBREVIATIONS

BLO – back loop only
ch(s) – chain(s)
hdc – half double crochet
inc – increase
invdec – invisible decrease
mr – magic ring
R – round or row
sc – single crochet
st(s) – stitch(es)
[...] – repeat the instructions inside the square brackets
(...) – indicates the stitch count at the end of the round or row

GAUGE/TENSION

Gauge is not important in this pattern. Use a hook size to match your chosen yarn and make sure that your stitches are tight enough to prevent stuffing showing through. Adjust hook size if necessary.

MALLARD DUCK

Using dark green yarn, make a magic ring.

R1: 6 sc in mr (6)
R2: [Inc] x6 (12)
R3: [Sc, inc] x6 (18)
R4: Sc, inc, [2 sc, inc] x5, sc (24)
R5: [3 sc, inc] x6 (30)
R6–10: [Sc] x30 (30)
5 rounds

Change to white yarn in the last stitch of R10.

R11: 2 sc, inc, [4 sc, inc] x5, 2 sc (36)

Change to dark brown yarn in the last stitch of R11.

Position the safety eyes between R8 and R9, 5 sts apart. Fix in place.

R12–17: [Sc] x36 (36)
6 rounds
R18: 2 sc, invdec, [4 sc, invdec] x5, 2 sc (30)
R19: [3 sc, invdec] x6 (24)

Start stuffing and continue to stuff as you work.

R20: Sc, invdec, [2 sc, invdec] x5, sc (18)
R21: [Sc, invdec] x6 (12)
R22: [Invdec] x6 (6)

Cut the working yarn, leaving a long tail. Pull the yarn tail through the last stitch.

Weave the yarn tail through the front loops only of the final round and gently pull to close the opening.

Hide any yarn ends inside the duck.

WINGS (MAKE 2)

Using dark brown yarn, ch 4.

Working down one side of the ch – hdc in second ch from hook, hdc in next ch, 4 hdc in last ch.

Working down the other side of the ch – hdc in last 2 chs. (8)

Fasten off, leaving a long tail for sewing.

FINISHING DETAILS

Sew the wings to the sides of the duck's body between R12 and R13, approximately 3 stitches away from each eye.

Using yellow yarn, sew a beak between R8 and R9 approximately 2 stitches long, centred between the eyes, by making 3 horizontal stitches over the same 2 stitches.

MOUSE

This crocheted mouse is super-quick, super-easy and super-cute. It's made up of a raindrop-shaped body with simple extra details. When making the tail, you will practise crocheting in the back bump of the chain. For a more three-dimensional effect, you can use a wrap knot for the nose.

FINISHED SIZE

Approximately 3 inches (8cm) long by 2 inches (5cm) wide, not including the tail.

Size may vary depending on your gauge/tension and the yarn used.

MATERIALS

- Paintbox Yarns Cotton Aran or any other worsted/aran-weight yarn in light grey (Stormy Grey) and light pink (Blush Pink)
- 3.5mm (US E/4) crochet hook
- Pair of 8mm black safety eyes
- Polyester fibre filling or any other fire-safe toy stuffing
- Stitch marker
- Scissors
- Yarn needle

PATTERN NOTES

• This pattern is worked in the round in a continuous spiral.

• Mark the first stitch of each round with a movable stitch marker.

• The tail is worked in the back bump of the chain.

GAUGE/TENSION

Gauge is not important in this pattern. Use a hook size to match your chosen yarn and make sure that your stitches are tight enough to prevent stuffing showing through. Adjust hook size if necessary.

ABBREVIATIONS

ch – chain
inc – increase
invdec – invisible decrease
mr – magic ring
R – round or row
sc – single crochet
sl st – slip stitch

st(s) – stitch(es)
[...] – repeat the instructions inside the square brackets
(...) – indicates the stitch count at the end of the round or row

MOUSE

Using light grey yarn, make a magic ring.

R1: 6 sc in mr (6)
R2: [Sc] x6 (6)
R3: [Inc] x6 (12)
R4: [Sc] x12 (12)
R5: [Sc, inc] x6 (18)
R6: [Sc] x18 (18)
R7: Sc, inc, [2 sc, inc] x5, sc (24)
R8: [Sc] x24 (24)
R9: [3 sc, inc] x6 (30)
R10: [Sc] x30 (30)
R11: 2 sc, inc, [4 sc, inc] x5, 2 sc (36)

Position the safety eyes between R6 and R7, 5 sts apart. Fix in place.

R12–17: [Sc] x36 (36)
6 rounds
R18: 2 sc, invdec, [4 sc, invdec] x5, 2 sc (30)
R19: [3 sc, invdec] x6 (24)

Start stuffing and continue to stuff as you work.

R20: Sc, invdec, [2 sc, invdec] x5, sc (18)
R21: [Sc, invdec] x6 (12)
R22: [Invdec] x6 (6)

Cut the working yarn, leaving a long tail. Pull the yarn tail through the last stitch.

Weave the yarn tail through the front loops only of the final round and gently pull to close the opening.

Hide any yarn ends inside the mouse.

EARS (MAKE 2)

Using light grey yarn, make a magic ring.

R1: 6 sc in mr (6)

Fasten off, leaving a long tail for sewing.

TAIL

Using light pink yarn, ch 25.

Sl st in the back bump only of the second ch from hook, and sl st in each ch across. (24)

Fasten off, leaving a long tail for sewing.

NOSE

Using light pink yarn, make a 6-wrap knot.

FINISHING DETAILS

Sew the ears to the top of the mouse between R9 and R10, in line with the eyes.

Sew the tail to the centre back of the mouse.

Sew the 6-wrap knot nose to the tip of the mouse between R1 and R2. Alternatively, sew a nose in light pink yarn using horizontal stitches.

TAKEAWAY COFFEE CUP

This takeaway coffee cup is a quick, satisfying make. It's worked from the bottom up in one piece and is perfect for practising working in the round, increasing and decreasing (both invisible and regular), changing colours, joining on yarn and half double crochet. It makes a great desk decoration, a cute gift for a coffee lover or even a fun pincushion.

FINISHED SIZE

Approximately 3 inches (8cm) tall by 2½ inches (6.5cm) wide.

Size may vary depending on your gauge/tension and the yarn used.

MATERIALS

- Paintbox Yarns Cotton Aran or any other worsted/aran-weight yarn in off-white (Champagne White), light brown (Soft Fudge), dark brown (Coffee Bean) and a small amount of pink (Bubblegum Pink)
- 3.5mm (US E/4) crochet hook
- Pair of 8mm black safety eyes
- Polyester fibre filling or any other fire-safe toy stuffing
- Card (you can use a cereal box, tissue box, etc.)
- Black embroidery floss/thread
- Stitch marker
- Scissors
- Yarn needle
- Embroidery needle

PATTERN NOTES

• This pattern is worked in the round in a continuous spiral.

• Mark the first stitch of each round with a movable stitch marker.

• All colour changes take place in the last yarn over of the previous colour.

• Round 6, Round 20 and Round 23 are worked in the back loop only.

• Regular decreases are used when working in the back loop only in Round 23.

ABBREVIATIONS

BLO – back loop only
ch – chain
dec – decrease
hdc – half double crochet
inc – increase
invdec – invisible decrease
mr – magic ring
R – round or row
sc – single crochet
sl st – slip stitch
st(s) – stitch(es)
[…] – repeat the instructions inside the square brackets
(…) – indicates the stitch count at the end of the round or row

GAUGE/TENSION

Gauge is not important in this pattern. Use a hook size to match your chosen yarn and make sure that your stitches are tight enough to prevent stuffing showing through. Adjust hook size if necessary.

COFFEE CUP
Using off-white yarn, make a magic ring.

R1: 6 sc in mr (6)
R2: [Inc] x6 (12)
R3: [Sc, inc] x6 (18)
R4: Sc, inc, [2 sc, inc] x5, sc (24)
R5: [3 sc, inc] x6 (30)
R6: Work the entire round in the BLO – [sc] x30 (30)
R7–8: [Sc] x30 (30)
2 rounds

Change to light brown yarn in the last stitch of R8.

R9: [Sc] x30 (30)
R10: [9 sc, inc] x3 (33)
R11–14: [Sc] x33 (33)
4 rounds
R15: 5 sc, inc, [10 sc, inc] x2, 5 sc (36)

Change to off-white yarn in the last stitch of R15.

Measure the diameter of the coffee cup base and cut a circle out of card the same dimensions. Place it inside the base of the coffee cup.

Position the safety eyes between R11 and R12, 5 sts apart. Fix in place.

R16–18: [Sc] x36 (36)
3 rounds

Change to dark brown yarn in the last stitch of R18.

R19: [Sc] x 36 (36)
R20: Work the entire round in the BLO – [sc] x36 (36)
R21: 2 sc, invdec, [4 sc invdec] x5, 2 sc (30)
R22: [Sc] x30 (30)

Start stuffing and continue to stuff as you work.

R23: Work the entire round in the BLO – [3 sc, dec] x6 (24)
R24: [Sc, invdec] x8 (16)
R25: [Invdec] x8 (8)

Cut the working yarn, leaving a long tail. Pull the yarn tail through the last stitch.

Weave the yarn tail through the front loops only of the final round and gently pull to close the opening.

Hide any yarn ends inside the coffee cup.

LID
Work the rim of the lid into the leftover front loops from R20 of the coffee cup.

Holding the coffee cup upside down, join dark brown yarn to the first leftover front loop from R20.

Ch 1, hdc in same space, 10 hdc, inc, [11 hdc, inc] x2. (39)

Fasten off invisibly to first hdc.

Weave in any yarn ends.

FINISHING DETAILS
Using two strands of black embroidery floss/thread, sew a V shape over R12 positioned between the eyes for the mouth.

Using pink yarn, sew a cheek just under and to the side of each eye by making two horizontal stitches over a single stitch.

HANGING CHERRIES

These crochet cherries are a fun, fast project that requires minimal sewing. You make two identical spheres for the cherries and then work more complex pattern instructions into a chain for the stem. But don't worry if each cherry turns out a slightly different size, it just adds to the handmade effect. You could use these as a handbag charm or a keychain to add a pop of colour to your outfit.

FINISHED SIZE

Approximately 4 inches (10cm) long by 3¼ inches (8.5cm) wide.

Size may vary depending on your gauge/tension and the materials used.

MATERIALS

- Paintbox Yarns Cotton Aran or any other worsted/aran-weight yarn in red (Pillar Red) and green (Grass Green)
- 3.5mm (US E/4) crochet hook
- Pair of 6mm black safety eyes
- Polyester fibre filling or any other fire-safe toy stuffing
- Black embroidery floss/thread
- Stitch marker
- Scissors
- Yarn needle
- Embroidery needle

PATTERN NOTES

- This pattern is worked in the round in a continuous spiral.
- Mark the first stitch of each round with a movable stitch marker.

GAUGE/TENSION

Gauge is not important in this pattern. Use a hook size to match your chosen yarn and make sure that your stitches are tight enough to prevent stuffing showing through. Adjust hook size if necessary.

ABBREVIATIONS

ch(s) – chain(s)
hdc – half double crochet
inc – increase
invdec – invisible decrease
mr – magic ring
R – round or row
rem – remaining
sc – single crochet
sl st – slip stitch
st(s) – stitch(es)
[...] – repeat the instructions inside the square brackets
(...) – indicates the stitch count at the end of the round or row

CHERRIES (MAKE 2)

Using red yarn, make a magic ring.

R1: 6 sc in mr (6)
R2: [Inc] x6 (12)
R3: [Sc, inc] x6 (18)
R4: Sc, inc, [2 sc, inc] x5, sc (24)
R5–9: [Sc] x24 (24) *5 rounds*
R10: Sc, invdec, [2 sc, invdec] x5, sc (18)

Position the safety eyes between R8 and R9, 5 sts apart. Fix in place.

Start stuffing and continue to stuff as you work.

R11: [Sc, invdec] x6 (12)
R12: [Invdec] x6 (6)

Cut the working yarn, leaving a long tail. Pull the yarn tail through the last stitch.

Weave the yarn tail through the front loops only of the final round and gently pull to close.

Hide any yarn ends inside the cherry.

STEM

The slip stitches are worked in the back bump of the chain, all other stitches are worked through the back loop of the chain as normal.

Using 3.5mm (US E/4) hook and green yarn, ch 30.

Starting in the second ch from hook, sl st in next 14 chs, [ch 5, sc in second ch from hook, hdc in next ch, dc in last 2 chs, sl st in same ch as last sl st back on starting ch, sl st in next ch] x2, sl st in rem 13 chs.

Fasten off, leaving a long yarn tail for sewing.

Gently stretch out the stem to loosen the stitches and shape the leaves.

FINISHING DETAILS

Using two strands of black embroidery floss/thread, sew a V shape over R9 positioned between the eyes for the mouth. Repeat for the second cherry.

Sew the stem to the top of the first cherry using the long yarn tail. Cut a separate length of green yarn to sew the stem to the second cherry.

ACORN

Autumn is all about cool weather, cosy vibes and comforting crochet projects. This cute acorn is a fun representation of the changing seasons. It's worked in three separate pieces using basic stitches that are assembled at the end. You could make a few of these to add autumnal décor to your home.

FINISHED SIZE

Approximately 3¾ inches (9.5cm) long by 2½ inches (6.5cm) wide, including the stem.

Size may vary depending on your gauge/tension and the yarn used.

MATERIALS

- Paintbox Yarns Cotton Aran in any other worsted/aran-weight yarn in light brown (Soft Fudge), dark brown (Coffee Bean) and a small amount of pink (Bubblegum Pink)
- 3.5mm (US E/4) crochet hook
- Pair of 8mm black safety eyes
- Polyester fibre filling or any other fire-safe toy stuffing
- Black embroidery floss/thread
- Stitch marker
- Scissors
- Yarn needle
- Embroidery needle

PATTERN NOTES

• This pattern is worked in the round in a continuous spiral.

• Mark the first stitch of each round with a movable stitch marker.

GAUGE/TENSION

Gauge is not important in this pattern. Use a hook size to match your chosen yarn and make sure that your stitches are tight enough to prevent stuffing showing through. Adjust hook size if necessary.

ABBREVIATIONS

ch(s) – chain(s)
dc – double crochet
hdc – half double crochet
inc – increase
invdec – invisible decrease
mr – magic ring
R – round or row
sc – single crochet
sl st – slip stitch
st(s) – stitch(es)
[...] – repeat the instructions inside the square brackets
(...) – indicates the stitch count at the end of the round or row

ACORN

Using light brown yarn, make a magic ring.

R1: 6 sc in mr (6)
R2: [Sc] x6 (6)
R3: [Inc] x6 (12)
R4: [Sc, inc] x6 (18)
R5: Sc, inc, [2 sc, inc] x5, sc (24)
R6: [3 sc, inc] x6 (30)
R7: 2 sc, inc, [4 sc, inc] x5, 2 sc (36)
R8–16: [Sc] x36 (36)
9 rounds

Position the safety eyes between R9 and R10, 5 sts apart. Fix in place.

R17: 2 sc, invdec, [4 sc, invdec] x5, 2 sc (30)
R18: [3 sc, invdec] x6 (24)

Start stuffing and continue to stuff as you work.

R19: Sc, invdec, [2 sc, invdec] x5, sc (18)
R20: [Sc, invdec] x6 (12)
R21: [Invdec] x6 (6)

Cut the working yarn, leaving a long tail. Pull the yarn tail through the last stitch.

Weave the yarn tail through the front loops only of the final round and gently pull to close the opening.

Hide any yarn ends inside the acorn.

ACORN CAP

Using dark brown yarn, make a magic ring.

R1: 6 sc in mr (6)
R2: [Inc] x6 (12)
R3: [Sc, inc] x6 (18)
R4: Sc, inc, [2 sc, inc] x5, sc (24)
R5: [3 sc, inc] x6 (30)
R6: 2 sc, inc, [4 sc, inc] x5, 2 sc (36)
R7: [11 sc, inc] x3 (39)
R8–10: [Sc] x39 (39)
3 rounds

Fasten off invisibly, leaving a long tail for sewing.

> **TIP**
>
> Keep trying the cap on the acorn as you work to check the fit. Once finished, the bottom edge should sit over R14 for the acorn. Adjust the number of rounds worked for the cap as required to achieve the correct fit.

STEM

Using dark brown yarn, ch 6.

Dc in 2nd ch from hook, hdc in next ch, sc in next, sl st in last 2 chs. (5)

Fasten off, leaving a long yarn tail for sewing.

FINISHING DETAILS

Place the cap on top of the acorn. The bottom edge of the cap should sit over R14 of the acorn. Sew the cap to the acorn using the method for sewing a flat piece to a closed piece (see page 79).

Sew the stem to the top of the acorn cap.

Using two strands of black embroidery floss/thread, sew a V shape over R9 positioned between the eyes for the mouth.

Using pink yarn, sew a cheek just under and to the side of each eye by making two horizontal stitches over a single stitch.

ICE CREAM CONE

This ice cream cone is a fun summer project that can be easily customized to make your favourite flavours. It's worked in one piece from the top down with alternating rounds of single crochet and decrease rounds to create the cone shape. The addition of the flake is optional, or why not try adding a few tiny multi-coloured stitches for sprinkles or brown knots for chocolate chips instead.

FINISHED SIZE

Approximately 4 inches (10cm) tall by 2½ inches (6.5cm) wide, not including the flake.

Size may vary depending on your gauge/tension and the yarn used.

MATERIALS

- Paintbox Yarns Cotton Aran or any other worsted/aran-weight yarn in light pink (Blush Pink), beige (Light Caramel), dark brown (Coffee Bean) and a small amount of pink (Bubblegum Pink)
- 3.5mm (US E/4) crochet hook
- Pair of 8mm black safety eyes
- Polyester fibre filling or any other fire-safe toy stuffing
- Black embroidery floss/thread
- Stitch marker
- Scissors
- Yarn needle
- Embroidery needle

PATTERN NOTES

• This pattern is worked in the round in a continuous spiral.

• Mark the first stitch of each round with a movable stitch marker.

• All colour changes take place in the last yarn over of the previous colour.

• Round 13 is worked in the back loop only.

GAUGE/TENSION

Gauge is not important in this pattern. Use a hook size to match your chosen yarn and make sure that your stitches are tight enough to prevent stuffing showing through. Adjust hook size if necessary.

ABBREVIATIONS

BLO – back loop only
ch – chain
hdc – half double crochet
inc – increase
invdec – invisible decrease
mr – magic ring
R – round or row
sc – single crochet
sl st – slip stitch
st(s) – stitch(es)
[…] – repeat the instructions inside the brackets
(…) – indicates the stitch count at the end of the round or row

ICE CREAM

Using light pink yarn, make a magic ring.

R1: 6 sc in mr (6)
R2: [Inc] x6 (12)
R3: [Sc, inc] x6 (18)
R4: Sc, inc, [2 sc, inc] x5, sc (24)
R5: [3 sc, inc] x6 (30)
R6: 2 sc, inc, [4 sc, inc] x5, 2 sc (36)
R7–12: [Sc] x36 (36) 6 rounds

Change to beige yarn in the last stitch of R12.

R13: The entire round is worked in the BLO – [sc] x36 (36)
R14: [Sc] x36 (36)

Position the safety eyes between R9 and R10, 5 sts apart. Fix in place.

R15: 2 sc, invdec, [4 sc, invdec] x5, 2 sc (30)
R16–17: [Sc] x30 (30) 2 rounds
R18: [3 sc, invdec] x6 (24)
R19–20: [Sc] x24 (24) 2 rounds

Start stuffing and continue to stuff as you work.

R21: Sc, invdec, [2 sc, invdec] x5, sc (18)
R22–23: [Sc] x18 (18) 2 rounds
R24: [Sc, invdec] x6 (12)
R25–26: [Sc] x12 (12) 2 rounds
R27: [Invdec] x6 (6)

Cut the working yarn, leaving a long tail. Pull the yarn tail through the last stitch.

Weave the yarn tail through the front loops only of the final round and gently pull to close the opening.

Hide any yarn ends inside the ice cream.

DRIPS

Work the ice cream drips into the leftover front loops from R13 of the ice cream.

Holding the ice cream cone upside down, join light pink yarn in the first leftover front loop from R13.

Ch 1, [sc in next front loop, 3 hdc in next, sc in next, sl st in next 3 front loops] x5, sc in next front loop, 3 hdc in next, sc in next, sl st in last 2 front loops.

Fasten off invisibly to first sc.

Weave in any yarn ends.

FLAKE (OPTIONAL)

Using dark brown yarn, make a magic ring.

R1: 6 sc in mr (6)
R2: Work the entire round in BLO – [sc] x6 (6)
R3–6: [Sc] x6 (6) 4 rounds

Fasten off, leaving a long tail for sewing.

FINISHING DETAILS

Using two strands of black embroidery floss/thread, sew a V shape over R10 positioned between the eyes for the mouth.

Using pink yarn, sew a cheek just under and to the side of each eye by making two horizontal stitches over a single stitch.

Sew the flake to the top righthand side of the ice cream over R5 and R6.

BEE

This chunky little bee is adorable with its cylindrical, striped body and simple antennae and wing details. This project will help you get comfortable with colour changes and learn to crochet amigurumi pieces closed to create a clean edge for sewing the wings on.

FINISHED SIZE

Approximately 3½ inches (9cm) tall by 4 inches (10cm) wide, including the wings and antennae.

Size may vary depending on your gauge/tension and the yarn used.

MATERIALS

- Paintbox Yarns Cotton Aran or any other worsted/aran-weight yarn in yellow (Buttercup Yellow), black (Pure Black) and off-white (Champagne White)
- 3.5mm (US E/4) crochet hook
- Pair of 8mm black safety eyes
- Polyester fibre filling or any other fire-safe toy stuffing
- Black embroidery floss/thread
- Stitch marker
- Scissors
- Yarn needle
- Embroidery needle

PATTERN NOTES

• This pattern is worked in the round in a continuous spiral.

• Mark the first stitch of each round with a movable stitch marker.

• All colour changes take place in the last yarn over of the previous colour.

GAUGE/TENSION

Gauge is not important in this pattern. Use a hook size to match your chosen yarn and make sure that your stitches are tight enough to prevent stuffing showing through. Adjust hook size if necessary.

ABBREVIATIONS

ch(s) – chain(s)
hdc – half double crochet
inc – increase
invdec – invisible decrease
mr – magic ring
R – round or row
rem – remaining
sc – single crochet
sl st – slip stitch
st(s) – stitch(es)
[...] – repeat the instructions inside the square brackets
(...) – indicates the stitch count at the end of the round or row

BEE

Using yellow yarn, make a magic ring.

R1: 6 sc in mr (6)
R2: [Inc] x6 (12)
R3: [Sc, inc] x6 (18)
R4: Sc, inc, [2 sc, inc] x5, sc (24)
R5: [3 sc, inc] x6 (30)
R6: 2 sc, inc, [4 sc, inc] x5, 2 sc (36)
R7–12: [Sc] x36 (36)
6 rounds

Change to black yarn in the last stitch of R12.

R13–14: [Sc] x36 (36)
2 rounds

Position the safety eyes between R9 and R10, 5 sts apart. Fix in place.

Change to yellow yarn in the last stitch of R14.

R15–16: [Sc] x36 (36)
2 rounds

Change to black yarn in the last stitch of R16.

R17–18: [Sc] x36 (36)
2 rounds

Change to yellow yarn in the last stitch of R18.

R19: [Sc] x36 (36)
R20: 2 sc, invdec, [4 sc, invdec] x5, 2 sc (30)
R21: [3 sc, invdec] x6 (24)

Start stuffing and continue to stuff as you work.

R22: Sc, invdec, [2 sc, invdec] x5, sc (18)
R23: [Sc, invdec] x6 (12)
R24: [Invdec] x6 (6)

Cut the working yarn, leaving a long tail. Pull the yarn tail through the last stitch.

Weave the yarn tail through the front loops only of the final round and gently pull to close the opening.

Hide any yarn ends inside the bee.

pattern continued

WINGS (MAKE 2)
Using off-white yarn.

R1: 6 sc in mr (6)
R2: [Inc] x6 (12)
R3: [Sc, inc] x6 (18)
R4–6: [Sc] x18 (18) *3 rounds*
R7: [Sc, invdec] x6 (12)
R8: [Sc] x12 (12)
R9: Sc, invdec, [2 sc, invdec] x2, sc (9)

Do not stuff.

With your crochet hook in the corner, press the opening together and work 4 sc through both sides to close (4)

Fasten off, leaving a long tail for sewing.

ANTENNAE (MAKE 2)
Using black yarn, ch 4.

Hdc in 2nd ch from hook, sl st in rem 2 chs. (3)

Fasten off, leaving a long tail for sewing.

FINISHING DETAILS
Position the wings so 6 rounds of each wing are visible when looking at the bee from the front. Sew the wings to the back of the bee over R12–15 with a space of approximately 2 stitches in between each wing.

Make an additional stitch to secure the wings to the body through the front of the wing only, approximately 7–8 rounds down from the tip of each wing.

Weave in any yarn ends.

Sew the antennae to the top of the bee over R4, approximately in line with the eyes.

Using two strands of black embroidery floss/thread, sew a V shape over R10 positioned between the eyes for the mouth.

OCTOPUS

One of the first amigurumi projects I ever made was an octopus. It seems to be a rite of passage for many new crocheters. This small octopus is worked in one piece from the top down and uses a variety of different stitches to create the curly tentacles. The tiny starfish is optional but I think it adds the perfect finishing touch.

FINISHED SIZE

Approximately 2½ inches (6.5cm) tall by 2¾ inches (7cm) wide.

Size may vary depending on your gauge/tension and the yarn used.

MATERIALS

- Paintbox Yarns Cotton Aran or any other worsted/aran-weight yarn in purple (Tea Rose) and light yellow (Daffodil Yellow)
- 3.5mm (US E/4) crochet hook
- Pair of 8mm black safety eyes
- Polyester fibre filling or any other fire-safe toy stuffing
- Black embroidery floss/thread
- Stitch marker
- Scissors
- Yarn needle
- Embroidery needle

PATTERN NOTES

• This pattern is worked in the round in a continuous spiral.

• Mark the first stitch of each round with a movable stitch marker.

• Round 18 is worked into the front loop only.

• Regular decreases are used when working Round 19.

GAUGE/TENSION

Gauge is not important in this pattern. Use a hook size to match your chosen yarn and make sure that your stitches are tight enough to prevent stuffing showing through. Adjust hook size if necessary.

ABBREVIATIONS

ch(s) – chain(s)
dec – decrease
dc – double crochet
FLO – front loop only
hdc – half double crochet
inc – increase
invdec – invisible decrease
mr – magic ring
R – round or row

sc – single crochet
sk – skip
sl st – slip stitch
st(s) – stitch(es)
[...] – repeat the instructions inside the square brackets
(...) – indicates the stitch count at the end of the round or row

OCTOPUS

Using purple yarn, make a magic ring.

R1: 6 sc in mr (6)
R2: [Inc] x6 (12)
R3: [Sc, inc] x6 (18)
R4: Sc, inc, [2 sc, inc] x5, sc (24)
R5: [3 sc, inc] x6 (30)
R6: 2 sc, inc, [4 sc, inc] x5, 2 sc (36)
R7–12: [Sc] x36 (36) 6 rounds
R13: 2 sc, invdec, [4 sc, invdec] x5, 2 sc (30)
R14–15: [Sc] x30 (30) 2 rounds
R16: [3 sc, invdec] x6 (24)
R17: [Sc] x24 (24)

Position the safety eyes between R12 and R13, 5 sts apart. Fix in place.

The next round forms the tentacles. Work the entire round in the front loop only and mark the back loop of the first and last stitch with a stitch marker so you can easily identify them in R19.

R18: Work the entire round in the FLO – [sl st, ch 10, inc in second ch from hook, sc in next 2 chs, hdc in next 3 chs, dc in last 3 chs, sk 1, sl st in next st] x8

The tentacles will naturally curl, but you can also shape and position them with your hands.

Start stuffing and continue to stuff as you work.

The next round is worked in the leftover back loops behind the tentacles and both loops of the skipped stitches from R18.

R19: Sc, dec, [2 sc, dec] x5, sc (18)
R20: [Sc, invdec] x6 (12)
R21: [Invdec] x6 (6)

Cut the working yarn, leaving a tail. Pull the yarn tail through the last stitch.

Weave the yarn tail through the front loops only of the final round and gently pull to close the opening.

Hide any yarn ends inside the octopus.

STARFISH (OPTIONAL)

Using light yellow yarn, make a magic ring.

Working in the magic ring – [ch 3, sl st in second ch from hook, sc in last ch, sl st in magic ring] x5.

Fasten off, leaving a long tail for sewing.

FINISHING DETAILS

Sew the starfish to the top lefthand side of the octopus. The points of the star should sit approximately over R5–9.

Using two strands of black embroidery floss/thread, sew a V shape over R13 positioned between the eyes for the mouth.

CAT

This adorable cat is sweet and simple. You start by crocheting the head, which is then closed at the top to imitate ears before working the body off a round of leftover front loops. The facial details give it personality and the bow around the neck is the perfect finishing touch. Instead of using yarn for the bow, you could also use thin ribbon and even add a little charm as a pet tag.

FINISHED SIZE

Approximately 4 inches (10cm) tall by 2½ inches (6.5cm) wide not including the tail.

Size may vary depending on your gauge/tension and the yarn used.

MATERIALS

- Paintbox Yarns Cotton Aran or any other worsted/aran-weight yarn in light grey (Stormy Grey) and a small amount of light pink (Blush Pink) and blue (Washed Teal)
- 3.5mm (US E/4) crochet hook
- Pair of 8mm black safety eyes
- Polyester fibre filling or any other fire-safe toy stuffing
- Pipe cleaner/chenille stem
- Black embroidery floss/thread
- Stitch marker
- Scissors
- Yarn needle
- Embroidery needle

ABBREVIATIONS

BLO – back loop only
ch – chain
inc – increase
invdec – invisible decrease
mr – magic ring
R – round or row
rem – remaining
sc – single crochet
sl st – slip stitch
st(s) – stitch(es)
[...] – repeat the instructions inside the square brackets
(...) – indicates the stitch count at the end of the round or row

PATTERN NOTES

- This pattern is worked in the round in a continuous spiral.
- Mark the first stitch of each round with a movable stitch marker.
- Round 4 of the head is worked in the back loop only.

GAUGE/TENSION

Gauge is not important in this pattern. Use a hook size to match your chosen yarn and make sure that your stitches are tight enough to prevent stuffing showing through. Adjust hook size if necessary.

HEAD

Using light grey yarn, make a magic ring.

R1: 6 sc in mr (6)
R2: [Inc] x6 (12)
R3: [Sc, inc] x6 (18)
R4: Work the entire round in the BLO – sc, inc, [2 sc, inc] x5, sc (24)
R5: [3 sc, inc] x6 (30)
R6: 2 sc, inc, [4 sc, inc] x5, 2 sc (36)
R7–12: [Sc] x30 (36) *6 rounds*
R13: 5 sc, invdec, [10 sc, invdec] x2, 5 sc (33)
R14: [9 sc, invdec] x3 (30)
R15: 4 sc, invdec, [8 sc, invdec] x2, 4 sc (27)
R16: [7 sc, invdec] x3 (24)
R17: 8 sc to the corner, leave the rem sts unworked.

With your crochet hook in the corner, position the safety eyes between R10 and R11, 7 sts apart. Press the opening closed to double check their positioning before fixing in place.

Start stuffing and continue to stuff as you work.

With your crochet hook in the corner, press the opening together, 11 sc through both sides to close (11)

Add additional stuffing before closing completely, focusing on the two corners.

Fasten off.

Weave in any yarn ends.

BODY

Work R1 of the body into the leftover front loops from R13 of the head.

Holding the cat upside down, join light grey yarn in the first leftover front loop from R4.

R1: Ch 1, sc in same space, inc, [2 sc, inc] x5, sc (24)
R2–3: [Sc] x24 (24) *2 rounds*
R4: [3 sc, inc] x6 (30)
R5–9: [Sc] x30 (30) *5 rounds*
R10: [3 sc, invdec] x6 (24)

Start stuffing and continue to stuff as you work.

R11: Sc, invdec, [2 sc, invdec] x5, sc (18)
R12: [Sc, invdec] x6 (12)
R13: [Invdec] x6 (6)

Cut the working yarn, leaving a long tail. Pull the yarn tail through the last stitch.

Weave the yarn tail through the front loops only of the final round and gently pull to close the opening.

Hide any yarn ends inside the body.

pattern continued

TAIL

Using light grey yarn, make a magic ring.

R1: 6 sc in mr (6)
R2–15: [Sc] x6 (6) *14 rounds*

Do not stuff.

Take a chenille stem/pipe cleaner, fold it in half and twist together. Insert the chenille stem/pipe cleaner into the tail and trim off any excess.

With your crochet hook in the corner, press the opening together, 2 sc through both sides to close (2)

Fasten off, leaving a long tail for sewing.

FINISHING DETAILS

Using light pink yarn, sew a nose between R10 and R11 approximately 3 stitches long, centred between the eyes, by making 3–4 horizontal stitches over the same 3 stitches.

Using two strands of black embroidery floss/thread, sew a vertical line, 2 stitches long, down from the centre of the nose.

Using two strands of black embroidery floss, sew two whiskers just below and to the side of each eye.

Cut two strands of blue yarn approximately 12 inches (30cm) long. Hold the strands together and tie in a bow around the cat's neck. Trim off any excess to neaten.

Sew the tail to the back of the cat at an angle over R10. Bend it slightly away from the body. When you're happy with how it looks from the front, make another stitch approximately 5 rounds up the tail to secure it to the body.

FLOWER POT

This crochet flower pot would make a sweet desk buddy or gift – think house warmings, birthdays and anniversaries. The pot and soil are worked in one piece while the leaf and flowers are worked separately using a variety of different stitches and then sewn in place.

FINISHED SIZE

Approximately 2½ inches (6.5cm) long by 2½ inches (6.5cm) wide.

Size may vary depending on your gauge/tension and the yarn used.

MATERIALS

- Paintbox Yarns Cotton Aran or any other worsted/aran-weight yarn in terracotta (Vintage Pink), dark brown (Coffee Been), green (Grass Green), purple (Pansy Purple) and yellow (Mustard Yellow)
- 3.5mm (US E/4) crochet hook
- Pair of 8mm black safety eyes
- Polyester fibre filling or any other fire-safe toy stuffing
- Card (you can use a cereal box, tissue box, etc.)
- Black embroidery floss/thread
- Stitch marker
- Scissors
- Yarn needle
- Embroidery needle

PATTERN NOTES

- This pattern is worked in the round in a continuous spiral.
- Mark the first stitch of each round with a movable stitch marker.
- Round 7 of the pot is worked in the back loop only.
- Round 15 of the pot is worked in the front loop only.
- The leaf is worked around a foundation chain (see page 43).

GAUGE/TENSION

Gauge is not important in this pattern. Use a hook size to match your chosen yarn and make sure that your stitches are tight enough to prevent stuffing showing through. Adjust hook size if necessary.

ABBREVIATIONS

BLO – back loop only
ch(s) – chain(s)
dc – double crochet
dec – decrease
FLO – front loop only
hdc – half double crochet
inc – increase
invdec – invisible decrease
mr – magic ring
R – round or row
sc – single crochet
sl st – slip stitch
st(s) – stitch(es)
tr – treble crochet
[...] – repeat the instructions inside the square brackets
(...) – indicates the stitch count at the end of the round or row

FLOWER POT

Using terracotta yarn, make a magic ring.

R1: 6 sc in mr (6)
R2: [Inc] x6 (12)
R3: [Sc, inc] x6 (18)
R4: Sc, inc, [2 sc, inc] x5, sc (24)
R5: [3 sc, inc] x6 (30)
R6: 2 sc, inc, [4 sc, inc] x5, 2 sc (36)
R7: [BLO sc] x36 (36)
R8–14: [Sc] x36 (36) 7 rounds
R15: Work the entire round in the FLO – sl st to first sc, ch 2, dc in same st and in each st around (36)

Fold R15 down towards you until the leftover back loops are exposed.

Fasten off invisibly to first dc.

Weave in any yarn ends.

Measure the diameter of the base and cut a circle out of card the same dimensions. Place it inside the base of the flower pot.

Position the safety eyes between R9 and R10, 5 sts apart. Fix in place.

SOIL
Work R1 of the soil into the leftover back loops from R15 of the flower pot.

Join dark brown yarn to the first leftover back loop from R15 of the flower pot.

R1: Ch 1, sc in same space, dec, [2 sc, dec] x8, sc (27)

Start stuffing and continue to stuff as you work.

R2: [Sc, invdec] x9 (18)
R3: [Invdec] x9 (9)

Make an additional invdec (8)

Cut the working yarn, leaving a long tail. Pull the yarn tail through the last stitch.

Weave the yarn tail through the front loops only of the final round and gently pull to close the opening.

Hide any yarn ends inside the soil.

OPTIONAL
Holding the flower pot upside down, join terracotta yarn in the first leftover front loop from R7.

Ch 1, sl st in next front loop and in each front loop around.

Fasten off invisibly to first sl st.

Weave in any yarn ends.

LEAF
Using green yarn, ch 9.

Working down one side of the ch – sc in second ch from hook, hdc in next ch, dc in next 2 chs, tr in next 3 chs, 6 tr in last ch.

Working down the other side of the ch – tr in next 3 chs, dc in next 2 chs, hdc in next ch, sc in last ch.

Ch 2, sc in second ch from hook, fasten off invisibly to first sc.

Fasten off.

Weave in any yarn ends.

FLOWERS (MAKE 2)
Using purple yarn, make a magic ring.

R1: [Ch 3, 2 tr, ch 3, sl st in mr] x5

Fasten off, leaving a long tail for sewing.

FINISHING DETAILS
Arrange the leaf on the soil so the tip of the leaf overhangs the rim of the pot above the left eye. Using a separate length of green yarn, sew the leaf in place. Only stitch around the bottom edge where the leaf touches the soil.

Arrange the flowers so they slightly overlap and cover the top part of the leaf and most of the soil. Sew the flowers in place.

For additional detail, make two 5-wrap knots using yellow yarn and sew them to the centre of each flower. Alternatively, you can also use small buttons, beads or French knots.

Using two strands of black embroidery floss/thread, sew a V shape over R9 positioned between the eyes for the mouth.

BEAR

A teddy bear is a timeless, classic stuffed toy, which is perfect for gifting. For this project, you create a one-piece body by crocheting the legs together as well as practising some additional sewing techniques.

FINISHED SIZE

Approximately 5 inches (13cm) long by 3 inches (7.5cm) wide.

Size may vary depending on your tension and the yarn used.

MATERIALS

- Paintbox Yarns Cotton Aran or any other worsted/aran-weight yarn in light brown (Soft Fudge), beige (Vanilla Cream) and yellow (Mustard Yellow)
- 3.5mm (US E/4) crochet hook
- Pair of 8mm black safety eyes
- Polyester fibre filling or any other fire-safe toy stuffing
- Black embroidery floss/thread
- Stitch marker
- Scissors
- Yarn needle
- Embroidery needle

PATTERN NOTES

• This project is worked in the round in a continuous spiral.

• Mark the first stitch of each round with a movable stitch marker.

• Round 19 of the body is worked in the front loop only.

• Round 2 of the scarf is worked in the back loop only.

GAUGE/TENSION

Gauge is not important in this pattern. Use a hook size to match your chosen yarn and make sure that your stitches are tight enough to prevent stuffing showing through. Adjust hook size if necessary.

ABBREVIATIONS

BLO – back loop only
ch – chain
FLO – front loop only
hdc – half double crochet
inc – increase
invdec – invisible decrease
mr – magic ring
R – round or row
sc – single crochet
sl st – slip stitch
st(s) – stitch(es)
[…] – repeat the instructions inside the square brackets
(…) – indicates the stitch count at the end of the round or row

LEGS (MAKE 2)

Using light brown yarn, make a magic ring.

R1: 6 sc in mr (6)
R2: [Inc] x6 (12)
R3: [3 sc, inc] x3 (15)
R4: [Sc] x15 (15)

Fasten off.

Weave in any yarn ends on the first leg only.

Repeat R1–4 for the second leg but **do not** fasten off.

BODY

R5: Continuing on from the second leg – ch 3, join to first leg with a sc in the first st of R4, 14 sc around first leg, 3 sc along the ch sts, 15 sc around the second leg, 3 sc along the other side of the ch sts (36)
R6–15: [Sc] x36 (36) *10 rounds*
R16: 2 sc, invdec, [4 sc, invdec] x5, 2 sc (30)
R17–18: [Sc] x30 (30) *2 rounds*
R19: Work the entire round in the FLO – [sc] x30 (30)
R20: 2 sc, inc, [4 sc, inc] x5, 2 sc (36)

Start stuffing and continue to stuff as you work.

R21–28: [Sc] x36 (36) *8 rounds*

Position the safety eyes between R23 and R24, 8 sts apart. Fix in place.

R29: 2 sc, invdec, [4 sc, invdec] x5, 2 sc (30)
R30: [3 sc, invdec] x6 (24)
R31: Sc, invdec, [2 sc, invdec] x5, sc (18)
R32: [Sc, invdec] x6 (12)
R33: [Sc, invdec] x4 (8)

Cut the working yarn, leaving a tail. Pull the yarn tail through the last stitch.

Weave the yarn tail through the front loops only of the final round and gently pull to close the opening.

Hide any yarn ends inside the bear.

ARMS (MAKE 2)

Using light brown yarn, make a magic ring.

R1: 6 sc in mr (6)
R2–5: [Sc] x6 (6) *4 rounds*

With your crochet hook in the corner, flatten the piece and work 3 sc through both sides to close (3)

Fasten off, leaving a long tail for sewing.

pattern continued

EARS (MAKE 2)
Using light brown yarn, make a magic ring.

R1: 6 sc in mr (6)

Fasten off, leaving a long tail for sewing.

MUZZLE
Using beige yarn, make a magic ring.

R1: 6 sc in mr (6)
R2: [Inc] x6 (12)

Fasten off invisibly, leaving a long tail for sewing.

Using two strands of black embroidery floss/thread, sew a horizontal line of approximately 6 stitches across the centre of the muzzle for the nose.

Using two strands of black embroidery floss, sew an upside-down V shape just below the nose on the muzzle for the mouth.

SCARF
Using yellow yarn, ch 101.

R1: Hdc in second ch from hook and in each ch across (100)
R2: Work the entire row in the BLO – ch 1, turn, hdc in each st across (100)

Fasten off.

Weave in any yarn ends.

FINISHING DETAILS
Sew the muzzle to the head positioned between the eyes. It should sit approximately over R21–24.

Sew the arms to the front of the body between R14 and R15, 5 stitches apart and in line with the eyes.

Sew the ears to the top of the head over R29, approximately 5 rounds up from the eyes.

Fold the scarf in half. Place the bear face up on top with the loop on the righthand side. Bring the two ends over the bear and feed them through the loop. Gently pull to tighten the scarf around the bear's neck with the two ends positioned at the side. Adjust the folds so that the bottom layer sits just over the top of the arms and the top layer sits under the muzzle.

INDEX

abbreviations in patterns 23
acorn 124–7
acrylic yarn 15
additional materials 19
alternating increases and decreases 62
aluminium crochet hooks 12
amigurumi, defining 8–9
amigurumi pieces
    crocheting the pieces closed 66–7
    crocheting the pieces together 68–70
    fastening off a closed piece 75
    wrong side vs right side 27
aran cotton yarn 15
asterisks in patterns 24

back loop only (BLO) 64
bamboo crochet hooks 12
bee 132–4
BLO (back loop only) 64

cat 142–7
chain stitch (CH) 36
    counting chain stitches 37
    foundation chain 36–9
    joining amigurumi pieces with a chain between them 68, 70
    joining amigurumi pieces together 68–70
    for the turning chain 40
cheeks
    crocheted cheeks 96, 98
    French embroidered knots 88
    simple embroidered cheeks 86
cherries, hanging 120–3
children and safety eyes 19, 85
closed pieces
    sewing an open piece to a closed piece 78
coffee cup 116–19
colours
    changing colours 63
    yarn colours 17
cotton yarn 15
crochet hooks *see* hooks

cylindrical pieces
    crocheting the pieces closed 66–7

decrease (DEC or SC2TOG) 60
    alternating increases and decreases 62
double crochet (DC) 46–7
    turning chain length 42
double treble crochet
    turning chain length 42

embroidered knots 88–9
embroidery floss/thread 19
embroidery needles 19
    adding mouths 87
equipment 19
ergonomic crochet hooks 12
eyes
    embroidered knots 88
    safety eyes 19, 84–5
    simple embroidered eyes 85

facial details 84–9
    crocheted cheeks 96, 98
    embroidered cheeks 86
    embroidered eyes 85
    embroidered knots 88–9
    mouths 87
    noses 87
    safety eyes 19, 84–5
fastening off 73–5
finishing techniques 72–89
    facial details 84–9
    fastening off 73–5
    sewing 76–80
    stuffing 72
FLO (front loop only) 64
flower pot 148–51
foundation chains 36–9
    crocheting around a foundation chain 43
    double crochet 47
    front and back 37
    half double crochet (HDC) 44, 45
    inserting your crochet hook 37
    slip stitch 52

    treble crochet 49
    working single crochet into a foundation chain 38–9
foundation ring 36, 37
French knots 88
front loops
    front loop only (FLO) 64
    joining yarn in 65

gauge/tension 17
    in crochet patterns 26
    holding the hook 31
    yarn over (YO) vs yarn under (YU) 41

half double crochet (HDC) 44–5
    turning chain length 42
hanging cherries 120–3
hooks 12–13
    foundation chains 37
    holding 31
    inline hooks 12
    materials 12
    sizes 13, 17, 26
    styles 12
    tapered 12

ice cream cone 128–31
increase (INC)
    alternating increases and decreases 62
    working an increase 59
inline hooks 12
invisible decrease (INVDEC) 60, 61

jointed rounds 53

knots, embroidered 88–9

lemon 96–9

magic ring (MR) 55–8
mallard duck 108–11
metal needles 19
mouse 112–15
mouths, adding 87

needles 19
    embroidery needles 19, 87
    sewing needles 19
    yarn needles 19, 85, 86, 87, 88–9
no-sew patterns 76
noses, adding 87

octopus 138–41
open pieces
    sewing to a closed piece 78
    sewing two open pieces together 76–7

Paintbox Yarns Cotton Aran 15
parenthesis in patterns 24
patterns 21–6
    abbreviations 23
    acorn 124–7
    bear 152–7
    bee 132–4
    cat 142–7
    flower pot 148–51
    gauge-tension 26
    hanging cherries 120–3
    hook sizes in 26
    ice cream cone 128–31
    mallard duck 108–11
    mouse 112–15
    no-sew 76
    octopus 138–41
    pencil 100–3
    planet 104–7
    potato 92–5
    sample pattern 25
    sour lemon 96–9
    stitches and terms 23
    subheadings 26
    symbols 24
    takeaway coffee cup 116–19
    US vs UK terminology 22
    working in rounds 23
    working in rows 23
pencil 100–3
planet 104–7
plastic crochet hooks 12
polyester fibre filling 19
potato 92–5

rounds, working in 53
    changing colours 63
    continuous spiral 53
    counting rounds 54
    crocheting amigurumi pieces together 68–70
    fastening off 74
    jointed rounds 53
    reading a pattern 23
    wrong side vs right side 27
rows, working in
    fastening off 73
    reading a pattern 23
    single crochet 40

safety eyes 19, 84–5
SC see single crochet (SC)
sewing needles 19
sewing techniques 76–80
    adding embroidered knots 88–9
    adding wrap knots 89
    facial details 85–9
    sewing an flat piece to a closed piece 79
    sewing an open piece to a closed piece 78
    sewing a finished edge piece to a closed piece 80
    sewing two open pieces together 76–7
single crochet (SC)
    turning chain length 42
    working into a foundation chain 38–9
    working in rows 40
    yarn over (YO) vs yarn under (YU) 41
slip knot 43
    creating 32–3
    holding your yarn 34, 35
slip stitch (SL ST) 52
sour lemon 96–9
square brackets in patterns 24
stacked increases and decreases 62
stitch markers 19, 40, 54, 68
stitches 36–71
    chain stitch (CH) 36
    counting stitches after each row 40
    counting stitches and rounds 54
    double crochet (DC) 46–7
    foundation chains 36–9, 44
    half double crochet (HDC) 44–5
    practising basic stitches 30
    treble crochet (TR) 48–51
    turning chain (TCH) 19, 40
stuffing 72

tapered hooks 12
tapestry needles 19
TCH (turning chain) 40, 42
tension see gauge/tension
tools 19
treble crochet (TR) 48–51
    turning chain length 42
turning chain (TCH) 40, 42

US vs UK terminology 22

wooden crochet hooks 12
wrap knots 89

yarn 15
    changing colours 63
    colours 17
    fibre 15, 17
    joining in unworked front loops 65
    reading the wrapper 16–17
    substituting 17
    weight 16, 17
yarn needles 19
    adding noses 87
    embroidered cheeks 86
    embroidered eyes 85
    embroidered knots 88–9
yarn over (YO) vs yarn under (YU) 41
yarn tails 32, 33, 34, 35
    fastening off 73, 74
    magic ring 55, 57
    sewing techniques 76, 77, 78, 79
    starting 27
    weaving in yarn ends 81–3

Index 159

RESOURCES

Here are some online shops and resources that you might find helpful. Whenever possible, support your local yarn and craft store, which is also a great place to get in-person advice.

YARN AND OTHER SUPPLIES

LoveCrafts – www.lovecrafts.com
Hobbii – www.hobbii.com
Wool Warehouse – www.woolwarehouse.co.uk
WeCrochet – www.wecrochet.com

CROCHET HOOKS AND NOTIONS

Clover – www.clover-USA.com
KnitPro – www.knitpro.eu

SAFETY EYES

Glass Eyes Online – www.glasseyesonline.com
6060Eyes – www.6060eyes.com

CROCHET PATTERNS

Amigurumi.com – www.amigurumi.com
Etsy – www.etsy.com
Ravelry – www.ravelry.com
Ribblr – www.ribblr.com

First published in Great Britain in 2026 by Ilex, an imprint of Octopus Publishing Group Ltd
Carmelite House
50 Victoria Embankment
London EC4Y 0DZ
www.octopusbooks.co.uk

An Hachette UK Company
www.hachette.co.uk

The authorized representative in the EEA is Hachette Ireland, 8 Castlecourt Centre, Dublin 15, D15 XTP3, Ireland
(email: info@hbgi.ie)

Text copyright ©
Fay Lyth 2026
Design and layout copyright © Octopus Publishing Group Ltd 2026

Distributed in the US by Hachette Book Group, 1290 Avenue of the Americas, 4th and 5th Floors
New York, NY 10104

Distributed in Canada by Canadian Manda Group, 664 Annette St., Toronto, Ontario, Canada M6S 2C8

All rights reserved. No part of this work may be reproduced or utilized in any form or by any means, electronic or mechanical, including photocopying, recording or by any information storage and retrieval system, without the prior written permission of the publisher.

Fay Lyth asserts the moral right to be identified as the author of this work.

ISBN: 978-1-78157-970-1
eISBN: 978-1-78157-971-8

A CIP catalogue record for this book is available from the British Library.

Printed and bound in China.

10 9 8 7 6 5 4 3 2 1

Commissioning Editor: Emma Hanson
Editor: Scarlet Furness
Copy Editor: Lisa Pendreigh
Art Director: Ben Gardiner
Designer: Jane Lanaway
Illustrator: Caitlin Keegan
Photographer: Carolyn Robertson
Production Manager: Caroline Alberti